305.4

D1081341

PICTURE POST

WOMEN

PICTURE
POST
WOMEN

Juliet Gardiner

C&B
COLLINS & BROWN

Half title: *Members of the Ladies' Carlton Club*
Frontispiece: *Wartime dance hall*
Front jacket: *Fisherwomen discuss the price of fish*

First published in Great Britain in 1993
by Collins & Brown Limited
Letts of London House
Great Eastern Wharf
Parkgate Road
London SW11 4NQ

1 3 5 7 9 8 6 4 2

British Library Cataloguing-in-Publication Data:
A catalogue record for this book
is available from the British Library.

ISBN 1 85585 166 0 (hardback edition)
ISBN 1 85585 193 8 (paperback edition)

Conceived, edited and designed by Collins & Brown Limited

Editor: Mandy Greenfield
Picture Research: Juliet Gardiner
Art Director: Roger Bristow
Designed by: Ruth Hope

Filmset by Bookworm Typesetting, Manchester
Reproduction by Scantrans, Singapore
Printed and bound in Great Britain by The Bath Press

Contents

INTRODUCTION

THE COVER OF the first issue of *Picture Post*, which hit the streets on 1 October 1938, featured two exuberant women leaping in the air. The final issue, published on 1 June 1957, showed the same two women. It was appropriate, for in the nineteen years of its existence *Picture Post* held up a mirror to British society and, in the reflections in its pages, it was often women who held centre-stage.

Picture Post started publication just under a year before the outbreak of the Second World War. It was an entirely new sort of magazine, born of the convictions of the documentary film-makers of the 1930s that the ordinary was interesting, that everyone had a story to tell and that photographs should not illustrate a story – they *were* the story, with carefully chosen words used sparingly as a counterpoint and context.

The magazine was an immediate success. Its founding editor, Stefan Lorant, had promised its proprietor, Edward Hulton, that he could sell a quarter of a million copies of *Picture Post*: within a week it was selling a million copies, and within six months over a million and a half, and it was calculated that on average five people read each copy. It was only paper shortages during the war and afterwards that limited circulation.

The very act of reclaiming the ordinary meant that women found a place in the pages of *Picture Post* from the start. Once the camera left the traditional site of 'news' and started re-interpreting what was newsworthy as what was happening every day – rather than concentrating solely on great events and public lives – women were ensured a space alongside men.

For *Picture Post* was not just a recorder of events; it had an agenda – and the wherewithal to implement it. As Lorant wrote later, he came to 'recognize photography as a journalistic weapon in its own right, so that if – like myself at that time – you are determined to promote causes and affect conditions, photographs can be a potent means for doing so'. The magazine's agenda for women might echo Tennyson:

LEFT: *'A Little Circus Queen' (1949) – Ella Freeman, the youngest horse-ballerina in the country.* BELOW: *'I Want to be a Nurse' (1953) – Pauline Hill, a student nurse at the London Hospital.*

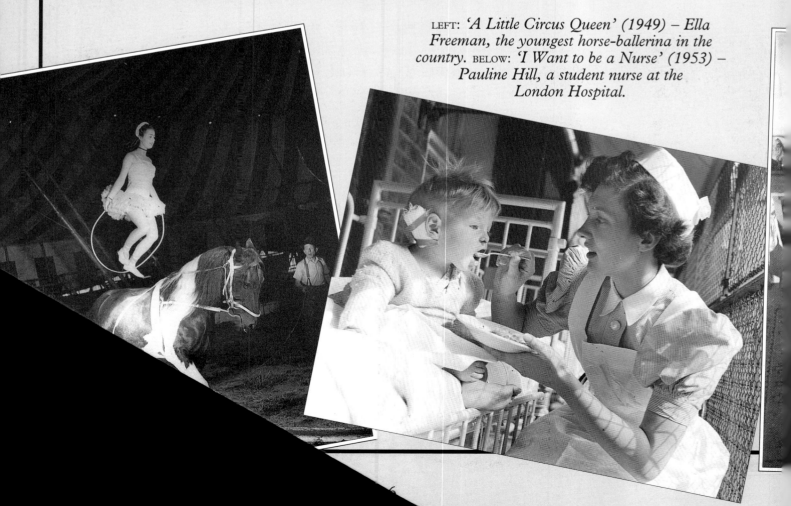

The woman's cause is man's:
They rise or sink together

in revealing Britain's unfulfilled promises to provide a 'land fit for heroes' of both world wars, its poverty, housing shortages, inadequate health care and lack of employment prospects, which impacted on both men and women. But its agenda also focused on women's 'separate sphere', sympathizing with the drudgery of housework, pointing out the need for better child care and nursery school provision, and the lack of facilities for working women in wartime.

But while sometimes campaigning for women, *Picture Post* also celebrated them, recognizing the diversity and richness of women's achievements and, in portraying their daily lives, it legitimized their right to recognition. 'Ordinary' women achieved an unprecedented visibility in the pages of the magazine, and just as the evacuation of city children in wartime had informed country-dwellers of another life, so did the stories carried in *Picture Post*. A day in the life of a woman lighthouse-keeper was described, as was the daily routine of the 'nippies', waitresses at Lyons Corner House. And the magazine featured women who married

GIs, Girl Guides, those who made slippers out of felt hats and necklaces out of beer-bottle tops, who operated barrage balloons, worked as chimney sweeps, bought nylon stockings on the black market, taught blind children, acted in amateur dramatics, were recruited to the Salvation Army, welcomed the liberating troops in France, did keep-fit exercises in cold church halls, made burdock wine and stewed garden nettles, fought for the right to play bowls on public greens, and nursed the mortally wounded, as they were flown back from the Normandy beaches.

But *Picture Post* did not just photograph women – it employed them, too. Anne Scott-James was appointed woman's editor in 1941 with a brief to cover 'women's issues', which she chose to interpret fairly widely. Distinguished women journalists contributed – Honour Balfour, Hilde Marchant, Venetia Murray, Katharine Whitehorn – and others wrote occasionally – Rebecca West, Vita Sackville-West, Antonia White among them. Its photographers included Merlyn Severn, who was on the staff from 1945–7; Gerti Deutsch, who arrived from Vienna in 1936 and freelanced for *Picture Post* from 1939–50; Grace Robertson, who started contributing

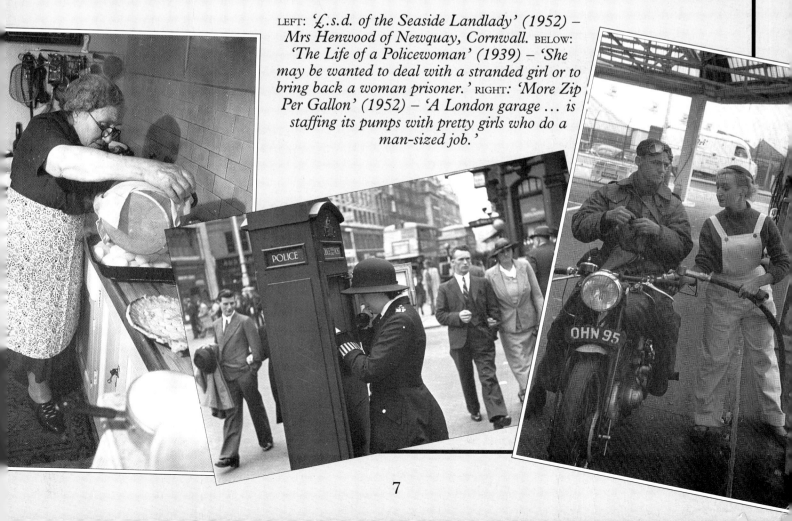

LEFT: '£.s.d. of the Seaside Landlady' (1952) – Mrs Henwood of Newquay, Cornwall. BELOW: 'The Life of a Policewoman' (1939) – 'She may be wanted to deal with a stranded girl or to bring back a woman prisoner.' RIGHT: 'More Zip Per Gallon' (1952) – 'A London garage … is staffing its pumps with pretty girls who do a man-sized job.'

photographs in 1951; and Edith Tudor Craig, whose photo-documentary work was perfectly adapted to *Picture Post*'s requirements.

Yet there was always an ambivalance about *Picture Post*'s treatment of women. On the one hand, the editor (Tom Hopkinson had replaced Stefan Lorant in 1940), the journalists and the photographers who worked on the stories – men like Bert Hardy, Kurt Hutton, Felix Mann, Thurston Hopkins, Haywood Magee, Slim Hewitt and Leonard McCombe – recognized that women hold up half the sky, and so when they explored the beaches of Blackpool, the slums of Glasgow, the pubs of Cardiff, they captured the women alongside the men. And it was bound to be the same in wartime. *Picture Post*'s war was a people's war, fought to a considerable extent on the Home Front, where women were in the front line too.

On the other hand, women were often objectified in the magazine as something to leaven the 'seriousness' of the social comment. 'Glamour' was brought to the pages with photographs of actresses, singers, chorus girls, cabaret stars, fashion models, artists' models, 'bathing beauties' and even corset mannequins. For a time the magazine chose a 'personality girl' every month, and frequently the cover picture bore no relation to any story inside the magazine, but was of a pretty girl – which could make *Picture Post* appear almost indistinguishable from most other offerings on the book stalls – which it certainly was not.

Not infrequently these two approaches fused, and a feature would demystify a star, claim the exotic for the ordinary and follow a chorus girl home to Mum in Yorkshire, show a 'professional dancing partner' scrubbing her kitchen floor, or praise a film star for drinking beer in a pub.

In the mid-1950s, in an attempt to increase its readership, which was flagging somewhat, *Picture Post* tried a succession of editors and of devices, too – including a series of '3-D' (three-dimensional) picture spreads. To enable readers to bring the pictures into focus, a pair of cardboard and celluloid glasses was stapled to the centre spread of the magazine. If you peered through these, the two disparate images merged – momentarily – to make a perfect whole. In this fractured and out-of-focus image, *Picture Post* provided a metaphor for understanding women's place and women's

LEFT: *'Day Trip to Boulogne' (1950) – Rank starlet, Diana Dors, 'was no sooner ashore than she was shanghaied on a French trawler'.* BELOW: *'Our Village Goes on a Nettle Hunt' (1942).*

wants at particular moments in the twentieth century – though the magazine ceased publication a few years before the decade in which women's demands for liberation began to be widely articulated.

Picture Post was of its time – how could it have been otherwise – and reflected the uncertainties about women's role in the post-war world. It worried about whether home-making would continue to be valued, and fought to preserve a rural way of life that seemed not to question such certainties; it asked whether women had 'justified the vote' that they had been granted in 1918, and assured its readers that by publishing a feature on unmarried mothers it was not condoning 'sin'. But in its unflagging wish to hymn the resilience of the human spirit, *Picture Post* was usually generous, and it was only rarely patronizing in its portrayal of women and their interests, at a time when 'feminist' was a word with which few women had currency – let alone applied to themselves.

* * *

Wherever possible, the photographers of the stories used in *Picture Post Women* have been named. Occasionally it has not been possible, however, to identify exactly who took the pictures: in the early days of *Picture Post* neither photographers nor writers got a byline for their work. Sometimes a feature was the work of more than one photographer, which can make accurate attribution difficult; many of the photographs taken for the magazine never appeared at all. Each photographer would shoot more rolls of film than could be used and many features were 'killed' at the last moment. Many of these photographs are too fine never to have been seen, and so this book contains not only work published in *Picture Post* but also 'overs' and previously unpublished material.

In writing this book, I am most grateful to Bert and Sheila Hardy, Thurston Hopkins, Gavin Lyall, Grace Robertson, Anne Scott-James and Katharine Whitehorn for talking to me about their work for *Picture Post*. I am also greatly indebted for their help to Derrick Brown, Matthew Butson, Brian Doherty, Steve Eason, Sandra Greatorex, Mandy McKenna, Donald O'Connor, Harriet Orr and Mark Syring at the Hulton Deutsch Picture Collection, which holds the *Picture Post* archive; and to Mandy Greenfield and Ruth Hope at Collins & Brown.

Juliet Gardiner
May 1993

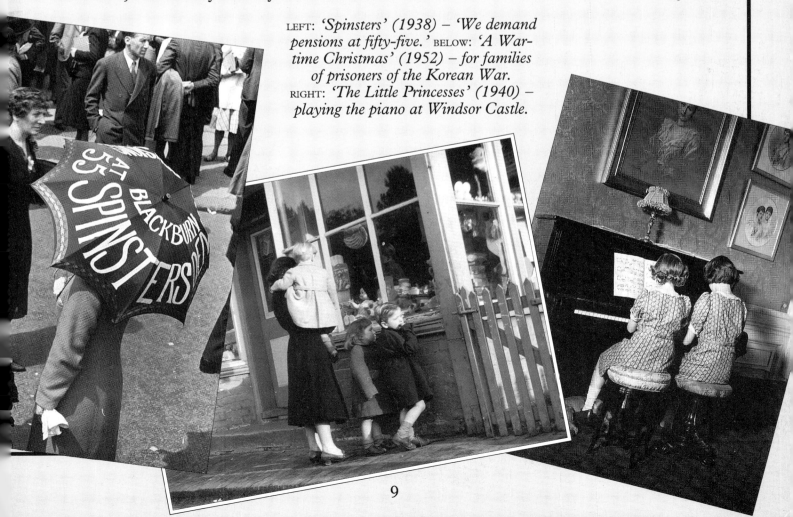

LEFT: *'Spinsters' (1938) – 'We demand pensions at fifty-five.'* BELOW: *'A Wartime Christmas' (1952) – for families of prisoners of the Korean War.*
RIGHT: *'The Little Princesses' (1940) – playing the piano at Windsor Castle.*

PICTURE
POST

July 3, 1943

CHERRY HARVEST

HULTON'S
NATIONAL
WEEKLY

In this issue :

HOW PANTELLARIA FELL

JULY 3, 1943

Vol. 20. No. 1

4d

EVERYDAY LIFE

DAILY LIVES have a continuum. Their fascination lies in the fixed moment and the unchanging quality. In its coverage of women's daily lives, perhaps more than in any other aspect of the magazine, *Picture Post* made memorable the supposedly quotidian: buying hats, getting married, being tall, gardening, partying – and keeping alligators in the bath.

Picture Post's position was explicit from the start. The magazine began to publish letters from readers a couple of months after its first issue in October 1938, and the very first letter that it printed was an attack on *Picture Post*. A Mr William Freeman of the National Liberal Club wrote that he was:

> moved to astonishment at the presentation week after week of pages and pages of totally unknown, totally undistinguished and, worst of all, totally uninteresting people, plus the added infliction of the photos being repulsively inartistic. These photos are the reason for my dropping the magazine for which I foresaw a magnificent future.

Picture Post's editor, Stefan Lorant, must have been delighted. The magazine might have forfeited Mr Freeman's weekly 3d, but it had been given the perfect opportunity to articulate its aims and intentions.

> This is a vital point at issue. Picture Post firmly believes in the ordinary man and woman; thinks they have had no fair share in picture journalism; believes their faces are more striking, their lives and doings more full of interest, than those of people whose faces and activities cram the ordinary picture papers. This goes for dictators and débutantes equally.

In fact, for the nineteen years of its existence, *Picture Post* did not neglect to portray either dictators or débutantes – or statesmen, politicians, film stars or aristocrats for that matter. But it did keep its promise to demonstrate that 'ordinary men and women's ... lives and doings are ... full of interest'. On such occasions this meant that *Picture Post* started with the people and found whatever story they had to tell. It meant that the agenda of 'news' had to be rewritten. As in documentary films, the response to the ordinary became complex. Was it so compelling because it merged stories and readers into the same narrative? Or was it that by photographing aspects of daily life it became possible to isolate them and to recognize the extraordinariness of the ordinary, as artists such as Andy Warhol were to do decades later?

11

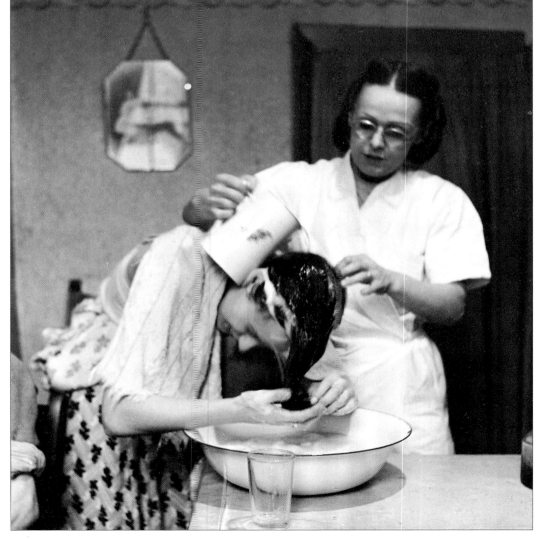

ABOVE: *Betty Burden works as a children's hairdresser in a Birmingham department store, as she has since she left school at fifteen. She hands her earnings of thirty shillings a week to her mother for board and lodging, and keeps her tips for herself.*
LEFT: *The hairdresser has her hair washed. A Sunday ritual in the front room, where her father is peeling potatoes for dinner and her sister and brother see to the Brussels sprouts.*

Millions like her

In 1951 Hilde Marchant and Bert Hardy went to Birmingham in search of a quintessentially 'ordinary' girl – not 'one in a million', but one of the millions of young women living and working in industrial Britain. They eschewed 'the imagined creature the sociologists write about' and found 'the real thing', 17-year-old Betty Burden, working as a hairdresser in a Birmingham department store. In celebrating Betty's individual life, *Picture Post* also gave a plaudit to all the other young women of the new generation of post-war Britain.

ABOVE: *Sunday afternoon. Betty Burden and a neighbour's child enjoy 'the fresh air' on a nearby bomb site.*

Photographed by Bert Hardy

13

The Ladies' Carlton Club

When the then Conservative Prime Minister, Stanley Baldwin, opened the new premises of the Ladies' Carlton Club in 1928, he exhorted its members, 'For goodness sake be keen. Be keen about the government of the country, or about the LCC, or about the maternity services, or about education. Anything you like – but be keen ...' Soon after the end of the Second World War, the Ladies' Carlton had well over 2,000 members, and what they were indisputably keen about was the purpose of their club, which was 'to provide a central and convenient rendezvous in London for ladies who are willing to do all in their power to promote the interests of the Conservative and Unionist Party'. When *Picture Post* visited the club in 1947, the Conservatives were out of office and it was the Labour Party's Mr Attlee who was at Number 10.

ABOVE: *Politics by other means Bridge partners keep a keen eye on the opposition's play.*

Photographed by Kurt Hutton

RIGHT: *Top people read* The Times.

White weddings, dream weddings, wartime weddings

'Weddings are substantially alike,' declared *Picture Post*. 'There are forms in these things; at morning-dress-and-champagne-affairs, or blue-serge-and-brown-ale ones, there are the same bridesmaids and favours, hired cars and cake, photographs and family reunions.'
And over the years, and in very different circumstances, the magazine set out to try to prove the truth of its proposition.

East End wedding

When Ellen Newman married Alfred Whitbread at St Andrew's Church, Bethnal Green, it was a pretty thorough-going affair – at least as far as the bride and her family were concerned. The wedding started the night before, with Ellen and her sisters scrubbing out every room until 1 a.m. Then it was up early to prepare the food for the wedding breakfast, as friends and neighbours dropped by with congratulations. The bride's father went out to get his hair cut, and at two o'clock Ellen went upstairs to get dressed.

Photographed by Bert Hardy

ABOVE LEFT: *The bride, the bouquet, her wedding day.*
ABOVE: *'To Ellen and Alfred. Your future happiness.'*
LEFT: *From house to pub, and back again, the wedding party celebrates into the small hours.*

Married in Scotland
When the Earl of Dalkeith, who had been regarded as 'Britain's most eligible earl', married Jane McNeill in St Giles Cathedral, Edinburgh, in January 1953, 1,600 friends – including the Queen and Princess Margaret – were there.

Photographed by Bert Hardy and Haywood Magee

ABOVE LEFT: *The Royal guests arrive – they came up by train from Sandringham.*
ABOVE: *The bride, a former Hartnell model, wearing a diamond tiara, a dress of French lace threaded with silver mayflowers, and, so readers were told, seven petticoats.*
LEFT: *The receiving line. It takes the newly-weds an hour and a half to shake hands with all the guests. Over 1,000 workers from the Duke of Buccleuch's half-a-million-acre estate come – the bridegroom is his heir.*

A soldier gets a bride
Spring weddings were as popular in wartime
as in peacetime. Serving men who were
engaged tried to get leave around Easter.
Sergeant Philip Ernest Jones of the 1st
Hertfordshire Regiment was fortunate.

So on a Saturday in early April 1942, the
village of Sulhamstead in Berkshire had its
own wartime wedding, when Nina Payne,
whose family lived in the village, married her
sergeant at the fifteenth-century Church of
St Michael – and for a short time everyone
was able to forget that there was a war on.

ABOVE RIGHT:
*The vicar has a
word with the
bridesmaids before
the ceremony.*
RIGHT: *'Wilt thou
have this man to
thy lawful wedded
husband . . . ?'*

RIGHT: *Then it's
back to the house
for congratulations,
toasts – and the
food that the bride's
mother has spent
days preparing from
wartime rations.*

*Photographed by
Kurt Hutton*

A housewife argues with Harold Wilson

The war had been over for four years. Britain had been the victor, but the rewards of peace seemed a long time in coming – it sometimes seemed that post-war austerity had set in for good. In 1949 Harold Wilson was President of the Board of Trade in the Labour government. So *Picture Post* sent along a housewife, Mrs Lillian Chandler from Bexley Heath, to interrogate the politician on behalf of the wives and mothers of Britain.

Mrs Chandler: *I expect you know, Mr Wilson, that women are very worried about prices. Of course we understand that we can't have luxuries to the same extent as before the war . . . but there are certain things we can't do without. Things like shoes and clothes, and sheets and towels, and saucepans and furniture . . .*
Mr Wilson: *I'd like to point out that I'm a father myself. I've got two small boys. And I assure you that my wife wouldn't let me go for long without learning about the difficulties the mother and housewife has today . . .*

Mrs Chandler: *Take this utility vest I've just bought for my 2-year-old boy. I paid 3s 11d for it and I've had to buy it two sizes too large, because I know it will shrink as soon as I wash it. Even then the shop would only let me have one, because they said they were so scarce – and you know no child can manage on one vest.*
Mr Wilson: *There's a shortage of the machinery for making children's sizes in woollen goods. Then again, some of the best wools are very scarce, and we do try to get as good quality as possible in utility goods . . . from time to time we have complaints about the quality of utility, but I can assure you that without this scheme the quality would be much lower, and the price far above your purse.*

Mr Wilson: *Unless anything unforeseen happens, things should gradually improve during this year.*
Mrs Chandler: *I am glad to hear it, Mr Wilson. Perhaps soon I shall be able to buy the other vest!*

Photographed by Bert Hardy

Women into action

The year 1950 saw the first January sales since the end of clothes rationing. 'Sensational Reductions' were to be had in shops that were slowly beginning to return to peacetime plenitude – if not quite to peacetime quality. If shops drew up their battle plans well in advance, so did the customers: the queues started before dawn – wartime habits died hard – bargains were targeted and strategies plotted. Then dead on nine o'clock the doors opened . . .

Photographed by John Chillingworth

ABOVE: *'You* know *plum's your colour, dear. Always has been.'*

ABOVE: *'I'm going to take it. I know I shouldn't, but I am.'*

LEFT: *It's straight to the hats . . .*

21

The unromantic gypsies

A royal hunting forest, painted caravans clustered round a camp fire, the life of the open road – the perfect photo-opportunity for an idyllic view of Britain's gypsies. But to *Picture Post* this was not a romantic scene. It was evidence of the 'gypsy problem' – British prejudice and failure to provide appropriate homes and proper services for the 100,000 or so people of no fixed abode 'about to become England's own DPs' (Displaced Persons, refugee victims of the war, who wandered around Europe).

The photographer, Bert Hardy, took pictures of gypsy families over a period of two years – in 1949 in the New Forest (BOTTOM AND FAR RIGHT) where 'tucked away from the bird-watcher and the weekending stockbroker, hundreds of poor folk live in compounds, under Stone Age conditions'; in 1951 at Corke's Meadow, at St Mary Cray in Kent (MIDDLE AND TOP RIGHT), where urban sprawl had enclosed meadowland and left 300 gypsies living precariously on a site that the local county council intended to develop for industry. Hardy focused on families, and in particular on the women's struggle to bring up their families in such miserable conditions; but also on their strong feelings for family and community, and on their strategies for living.

Gracie comes back to Lancashire

On a wet day in November 1954, Gracie Fields came home. She brought her husband Boris with her on a visit from the blue skies of Capri, where they now live, to the greyness of Rochdale – and a tumultuous welcome. She was born Grace Stansfield in 1898, above a chip shop in Molesworth Street – there's a plaque on the sooty wall there now. She worked in the mills before becoming a singer, and now she's world-famous – and the only Freeman of the Borough of Rochdale who can hit a high C.

Photographed by John Chillingworth

ABOVE: *The town of Rochdale lines up to welcome 'Our Gracie'.*

ABOVE RIGHT: *The civic duties of a Freeman (or, properly, a Freewoman).*

LEFT: *Gracie sings at the Theatre Royal – everything from 'Oh What I'd Give Again to Live Again the Days When I Was Twenty' to 'Eee, the Artfulness, the Sinfulness, the Wickedness of Man' and 'Wish Me Luck as You Wave Me Goodbye'.*

BELOW: *Finally, at just before midnight, Gracie appears on the balcony and sings her encore, 'Sally'. The house goes wild.*

Six families live as one

In the immediate aftermath of the Second World War there was an acute housing shortage – and at the same time there were large country houses all over Britain that were empty and in danger of becoming derelict, with no one living in them They were going cheap – but the upkeep would not be. So two couples decided that now was the time to put into practice the theories they had had before the war about communal living. They advertised for others who were 'progressive in outlook, congenial company', had a sense of humour, and who could pay £7 a week to cover the mortgage, food, running expenses – and staff wages.

In early 1946 six families moved into a 14-bedroom, 7-bathroom house standing in 22 acres of land and prepared to share their lives.

ABOVE: *During the week, the men work in town.*
TOP RIGHT: *And the women work at home.*
MIDDLE RIGHT: *A shared experience at mealtimes. The women work a rota for taking care of the children, which allows each of them a child-free day a week.*
FAR RIGHT: *The families come together to vet an application for a new resident.*
RIGHT: *Domestic support for progressive living. Employed help washes up for six families.*

Photographed by Merlyn Severn

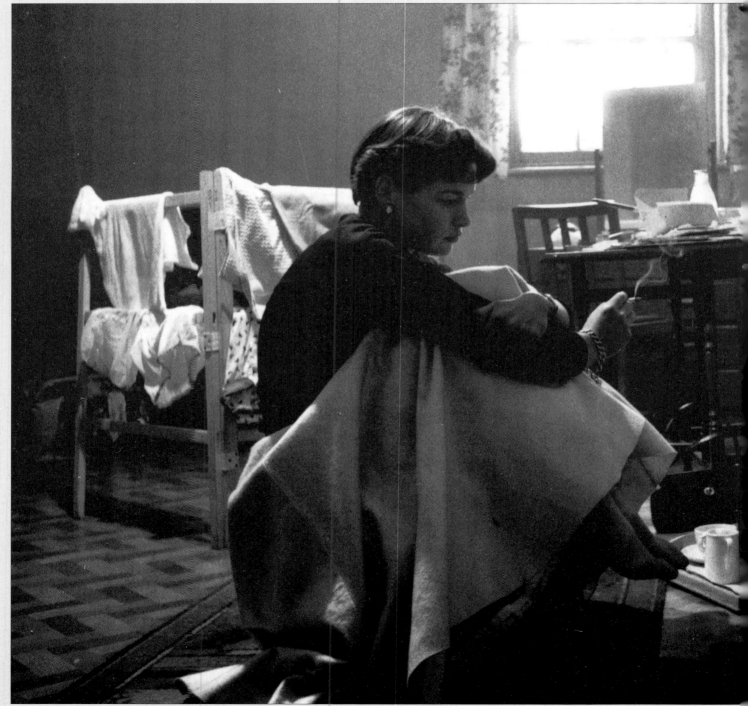

Katharine Whitehorn

Katharine Whitehorn joined the staff of
Picture Post in March 1956 – but she had
already figured anonymously in its pages. A
few years before Lynne Reid Banks's novel
The L-Shaped Room sketched the lives of
bedsitter-dwellers, *Picture Post* had decided
that this land of shilling-in-the-slot gas fires
was worth a visit. Girls who, before the war,
might have expected to stay at home and
help Mother until they married, were
venturing to the big cities in search of a
career – or at least a job – and independence.

Katharine Whitehorn was photographer
Bert Hardy's model for a feature in which
clever camera work isolated a 'girl from the
country' in the bustle of the metropolis to
illustrate the contention that 'loneliness is
particularly hellish in London':

> [where] eating out is expensive, where
> flats are small, and rooms are dreary;
> where distances are great and public
> transport dead at those hours when
> guests like to leave; where smog
> prevents you seeing other human faces
> in winter and where self-absorption
> prevents you seeing other human faces
> in summer; where people have no time
> for each other's problems.

Katharine Whitehorn had wanted to work
on *Picture Post* for as long as she had
wanted to be a journalist. 'Being a novice
journalist is like being a novice motorcyclist.
If you are in the sidecar, you want the
driver to be the best.' She learned how to
work with a photographer, and the skill of
marrying text with pictures. Her brief was
largely to report on 'women's interest
stories', so she visited a couple in Cornwall
who were going to take their baby around
the world in a ketch; investigated medical
claims in Sheffield; stood with footballers'
wives on a wet Whit Monday in
Manchester; and covered the Paris fashion
shows. And then suddenly it was over.
She had been at a press-conference for
Norwegian *sils* – 'a sort of fish'. The staff
were summoned to a meeting and the
closure of *Picture Post* was announced.

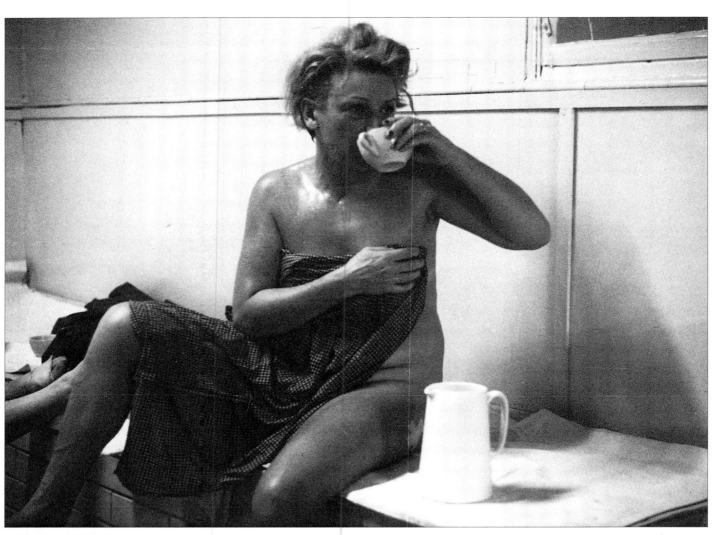

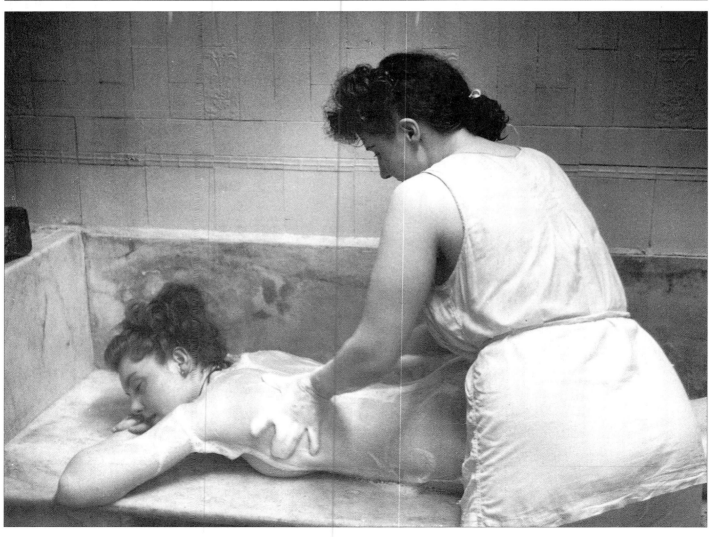

Ladies' Turkish baths

The photographer Grace Robertson and *Picture Post* writer Lorna Sage spent one foggy December afternoon in 1951 in the faded elegance of the Savoy Turkish Baths in London's St James's. They followed the regular clients of these Victorian ablution parlours from one hot and steamy room to the next, postponing the final ordeal – and the point of the whole exercise – a vigorous, cleansing pummel in the bath's marble wash-house, followed by a plunge into an icy-cold pool. Then it was on to the weighing scales and a massage, before venturing out again into the austerity of post-war London.

LEFT: *A women's club with a towelling-only uniform.*
BELOW LEFT: *A vigorous lathering on a marble slab with a wooden pillow.*
RIGHT: *Trepidation on the threshold of the first steam room.*
BELOW: *'Then you plunge into an icy pool . . !*
BELOW RIGHT: *'After all that, she hasn't lost an ounce.'*

Alligators and old lace

Miss Thelma Roberts and Miss Enid Davis live in a small cottage in Surrey. And they keep pets. But their pets are not the usual dog or cat – not even a budgerigar or a goldfish. Miss Roberts and Miss Davis share their lives with William, a 5-foot 6-inch-long alligator from China with a limp, and a female alligator that measures 7 feet from nose to tail and formerly lived in the waters of a Madagascar temple. She now lives in a galvanized tank, which takes up most of the kitchen – and for some reason she is called Peter. Then there's Peggy, who's an Egyptian crocodile aged four.

Photographed by Slim Hewitt

RIGHT: *Bathtime for William, who sustained a broken forearm during the London Blitz.*

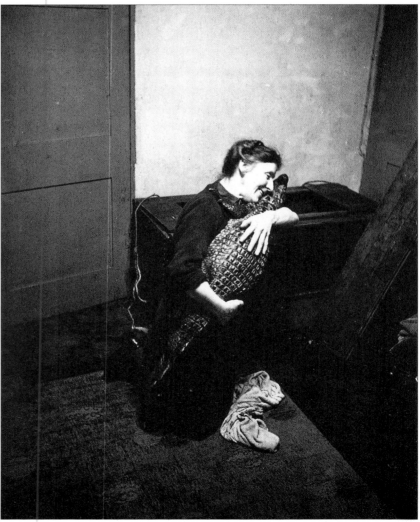

RIGHT: *Unlike her friend, Miss Davis has no professional interest in alligators – or crocodiles. She simply finds them lovable.*
FAR RIGHT: *The nights draw in and 'Peter', the 22-year-old alligator, hogs the fireside.*

ABOVE: *Backache – continual stooping over too-low sinks and ironing boards makes domestic chores twice as fatiguing.*
LEFT: *Stockings are never more than long socks for the tall woman, who often has long, extra-narrow feet, too.*
RIGHT: *A double-decker among the single.*

Problems of the tall girl

There were more than 2,000 members of the Association for Tall Women when *Picture Post* ran a story on them in 1952. In fact, the Association grew out of a letter that a Yorkshire woman had written to the magazine in 1949, pleading for manufacturers and retailers to recognize the problems presented by her size. The response was so enormous that the Association for Women with Big Feet was formed. But it was soon realized that it wasn't just feet that were the problem. Hence the name change.

The members ranged from a 15-year-old to a many-times-over grandmother and most stood between 5'10" and 6'5" tall. And all of them had one aim: to force manufacturers and shopkeepers to realize that tall women like nice clothes, just as their shorter sisters do.

Photographed by Grace Robertson

Down the Bay

Cardiff's dockland area's proper name was Bute Town. But it was often referred to as Tiger Bay and. with a population of Arabs, Somalis, West Africans, Afro-Caribbeans and Greeks, was all too often the scene of racial antagonism. In 1950, after riots in the area, *Picture Post* visited what the magazine described as 'the nearest thing we have to a ghetto in this free land'. It found that the women had to battle daily with insanitary and substandard living accommodation – 27 per cent of the houses had no indoor tap. There were few job opportunities for young women, other than working in local cafés or rag-picking factories – and they were often thought by outsiders to be prostitutes serving the seafarers who were in port.

TOP LEFT: *Not a patch of green in the area. Children play on the concrete oasis in the centre of Loudoun Square ...*

LEFT: *... and watch from the doorstep. They live in a community bound together by under-privilege, where the grocer's an Arab, the bootmender a Greek, where a sailor takes a drink in a Somali milk-bar or an Irish pub.*

Photographed by Bert Hardy

ABOVE: *Fighting against the damp, the women of Bute Town struggle to keep their homes clean and welcoming.*

RIGHT: *Kaid Sala's grocery store in Cardiff's dockland. Some 6,000 people live in Bute Town. 'It's an area with a bad name, but a decent heart.'*

The WI

Whoever thought the Women's Institute was only interested in making jam? The admiration that *Picture Post* had for the members of the WI – started on the Canadian model, in Anglesey in 1915, to 'bring a fuller life to the countryside, and through its members, to express the considered opinion of countrywomen' – knew no bounds. The magazine visited meetings and noted that 'the record of one WI is a record of the best of them. The story of a growing enthusiasm for the best in music, crafts and drama, co-operation in every kind of national effort is the same all over the country. Only the details vary.'

The members supplied produce for sale at markets – fruit, vegetables, flowers, rabbits, poultry, home-made cakes, cheeses and pickles (in 1952 the turnover was £77,608); they made music – the WI Singing Festival at the Albert Hall in 1950 was conducted by Sir Adrian Boult, a cantata was specially written by Vaughan Williams and fifty-nine choirs from thirty-five countries took part; members learnt to paint and draw, become expert needlewomen or basket-makers and to fashion leather goods. They opened their own

TOP LEFT: *'I shall not cease from mental fight, nor shall my sword sleep in my hand.' Blake's 'Jerusalem' is the national anthem of the WI. 'It expresses the members' resolve to work for a better Britain.'*
MIDDLE LEFT: *Time to cast a vote for the committee.*
BELOW AND BOTTOM LEFT: *The next item: tea. Two members of Groombridge WI in Sussex fetch the urn, and the cups are handed round.*
RIGHT: *Dancing at Eastgate WI in Weardale, Co. Durham (pop. 120). Some of the thirty-one members walk up to three miles across rough fell land to attend meetings. WI activities are their only recreation and, together with other Institutes in the county, Weardale branch has revived many old Durham folk dances.*

college, Denman College (named after the Federation's first president), in Berkshire in 1948, where members could take courses in quilting, rug-making, soft furnishings and much more besides; they lobbied the government on such issues as litter, undesirable comics for children, standard sizes in clothing, eye banks and bus shelters; they undertook a survey of rural water supplies, drainage and sewage disposal, covering over 10,000 villages – and found them sadly deficient; they studied local provisions for footpaths and byways in every county in England and Wales. In 1952 WI members published a report, *Child on the Road* – the result of a year's monitoring of child accident statistics. And they made jam – during the Second World War, the Ministry of Food handed over the entire fruit-preserving scheme in rural districts to the WI. The resultant orgy of bottling, canning and jam-making led to 2,000 tons of preserves being made in the summer of 1941 – a poor year for fruit – and fourteen hundredweight of this came from Hawkinge near the Kent coast, where bombing, fire and evacuation had reduced the WI membership to five!

Photographed by Kurt Hutton

Deb among the stags

Six hundred guests came to the actress Anna Massey's coming-out ball in her mother's garden on a perfect evening in the summer of 1955. The magnificent occasion had taken sixteen workmen days to prepare, and involved yards of imitation pearls, sixty specially dyed candles, two specially constructed bridges, 300 yards of muslin, thirty stags' heads, 250 pink carnations, 600 roses wired to a creeper-covered wall, and three cooks to prepare the fare. And what was the play that the young actress was currently starring in, in the West End? *The Reluctant Débutante.*

Photographed by Thurston Hopkins

Should women wear trousers?

The war put women in trousers. Doing jobs like lorry-driving, fire-fighting, portering – and even sleeping in a shelter – made it impracticable to wear a skirt. You can't fight a fire with confidence in clothes that flutter. But then women seemed to *like* wearing trousers, and soon they could be seen sporting them around town, too. Anne Scott-James, woman's editor of *Picture Post*, believed that most men hated them, so she sent a 'cameraman round the town to snap a bunch of trousered women' and asked the readers, 'Which of them d'you like?'

'Fascinated by their new competent appearance, women keep their trousers on in off-duty hours . . . '

PICTURE POST

April 3, 1948

A DEAF CHILD LEARNS TO SPEAK
(see inside)

HULTON'S NATIONAL WEEKLY

A New Idea to Increase Production:
WAGES ON POINTS

APRIL 3 1948

Vol. 39.   No. 1

4ᴰ

WOMEN'S WORK

As far as *Picture Post* was concerned, when it came to work there were women and there were mothers, and the boundaries were clearly drawn. Girls, or women, who were unmarried, had jobs – not often careers, but certainly jobs. Once they married, women's jobs became home-making and, in due course, motherhood.

The boundaries became blurred during the war, when government policy drafted women into war work. It was married women who made up the largest part of the labour reserve, and eventually two million of them combined jobs inside the home with war work. *Picture Post* ran various features on them working in war industries and filling the jobs of men away fighting: Honour Balfour, for example, sampled life in a Ministry of Aircraft production factory, and Anne Scott-James went to work for a day as a conductor on a Midland Red bus.

But when the men returned from war, married women found themselves back home again – and were encouraged to regard it as rather an affront to be required to work outside the home. As Anne Scott-James wrote in a stirring piece published in April 1947, 'The last straw is that "they" ['the officials who push people around'] want her to go to work in industry again on top of all her own work. The nerve of it!'

Picture Post exhorted women to stay at home to raise the next generation of home-makers, even though by 1956 it had recognized that motherhood is 'a job with a 100-hour week' doing work that 'should be classified as heavy industry – without overtime pay'. It was a losing battle. By 1951, 22 per cent of married women had jobs, compared with only 10 per cent before the war.

But the magazine's attitude towards single women was different. *Picture Post* had always welcomed their move towards economic independence and rejoiced in the diversity of the work they did. Jobs traditionally associated with women, such as teaching and nursing; newer jobs such as that of policewoman or petrol-pump attendant; feisty older women working as chimney sweeps, Members of Parliament or lighthouse-keepers; younger women doing unusual jobs, like being a wall-of-death rider or a rat-catcher – these were all seized upon as photo-opportunities. It was all slightly condescending, as if women made little impact on the male world of work, but by 1957 it might have been possible to discern that in the not-too-distant future things would be changing ...

A girl becomes an air steward

Even though a transatlantic flight took twenty-one hours, being an air steward – the term air hostess was frowned upon by *Picture Post*, which stressed the equality of work, conditions and pay of the men and women who did this job – was still much sought-after. Each week 150 women – compared to about fifty men – applied, but only three or four would be accepted for training. BEA, which came into service in August 1946, required its women stewards to be 'British by birth, have natural intelligence, a good education, the "right" kind of appearance, courtesy, a first-aid or home-nursing certificate and the ability to speak at least one Continental language' – and a domestic-science diploma or experience in the catering trade was 'a distinct advantage'. And there were overtones of the military: the women were forbidden to wear nail varnish and had to salute senior officers.

Photographed by Merlyn Severn

LEFT: *The training lasted for two to six months – 'depending on the adaptability of the girl'.*
RIGHT: *The steward has 'balance as well as poise. She is polite, but can be stern.'*
BELOW: *A passenger who prides herself on being 'such a good sailor' feels 'uncertain of herself', and requires a glass of water.*

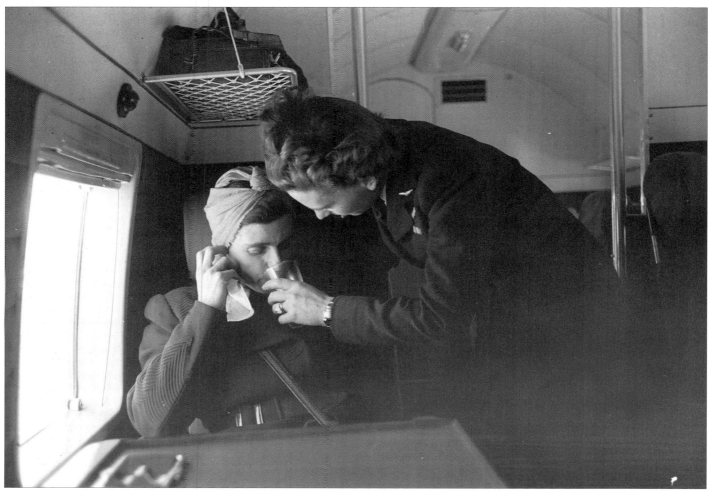

Bonjour tristesse

Françoise Sagan was just eighteen when she wrote *Bonjour tristesse* in 1954. The sophisticated story of love and Existential boredom in the south of France was one of the biggest literary successes since the war, selling over 350,000 copies worldwide in one year. It made a fortune for its young author, won literary prizes, and Hollywood bought the film rights. *Picture Post* went to Paris to photograph Françoise Sagan, since she seemed to epitomize Parisian charm in the 1950s – the Left Bank; black-clad, Gauloise-smoking intellectuals; cheap red wine drunk in cellar nightclubs; and perhaps a certain cynical *tristesse*.

Photographed by Bert Hardy

TOP LEFT: *Doreen Munns works on farms in Herefordshire and has an experienced eye for traces of rats – and an experienced nose for their presence.*

TOP RIGHT: *Grease-marks on stones are a tell-tale sign of a rodent's habitat. Doreen uses a long spoon to place the poison.*

ABOVE: *Success. Rats are wary creatures and so Doreen is careful never to use the same poison in the same place twice.*

RIGHT: *Hereford's female rat-catcher can bag up to a hundred rats in one day.*

Poisoner

Doreen Munns is a rat-catcher. The 25-year-old Liverpudlian learnt her trade in the Woman's Land Army and intended to carry on with it when the Land Army was disbanded in 1950.

Photographed by John Chillingworth

The 'herring lasses'

Every year in early October the 'herring lasses' migrate south. Following the drifters down from Scotland – Aberdeen, Lerwick, the Shetland Isles – the women work a 10-hour day on the quayside at Great Yarmouth, with the seagulls wheeling and screaming overhead, as they gut, grade, salt and pack some of the millions of herrings that are landed from the North Sea on to East Coast wharves throughout the 8-week season. It is hard and dextrous work – and it's in the blood. The girls who work with the fish come from families of 'herring lasses' – their mothers and grandmothers followed the trawlers too, and instilled in their daughters the rhythm of sorting and packing.

Photographed by Haywood Magee

RIGHT: *Calico strips protect the girls' fingers from the sharp gutting knives.*

RIGHT: *'It's nae work for a girl with a glass back.'*

FAR RIGHT: *The herring lasses work in teams – two to gut, one to pack.*

ABOVE: *The herrings are sorted in a trough called a farlane.*

LEFT: *'All you need is a good pair of hands, a good heart, an' a liking for a good day's work.'*

Anne Scott-James

'We Appoint a Woman's Editor,' triumphed *Picture Post* in February 1941. 'We have been urged for a long time to give some space to women's interests. We waited to find the right person to do the work.' The 'right person' was Anne Scott-James, former assistant editor of the fashion magazine *Vogue*. Nearly ten years later, after she had left *Picture Post* to return – briefly – to fashion journalism, Anne Scott-James wrote a parodic novel entitled *In the Mink*, in which *Vogue* became *Venus* and something rather like *Picture Post* was renamed *View*.

ABOVE: *Anne Scott-James in 1941.*
TOP RIGHT AND RIGHT: *'The woman's editor is fearless about the claims of cosmetics. In wartime they have to work for working women.'*
FAR RIGHT: *Checking out the ingredients for Woolton Pie to pass on to the readers.*

View was as different from *Venus* as bun loaf from angel cake ... Here first was a world of men instead of women. Here our subjects were war, politics, social problems, housing, work instead of fashion. Everyone on *View* had a mission in life, and a mission is apt to be distracting ... The Sense of Purpose started at the top ... several of the feature writers had missions too. They were always dropping their urgent war stories because they had heard of some dire political scandal: a left-wing allotment holder in Battersea dispossessed by a Fascist rival, or a malingering society girl wangled out of the ATS by an influential uncle at the War Office ... I myself soon entered into the swing of things and developed a fine indignant style of writing, in which I told the hospitals how to run themselves, the Food Ministry how to reorganize, the Army how to use its manpower, and the world at large how to build houses, care for children, reform the Zoo and supply Russia. I had a sound way of putting things, and my articles used to stir up plenty of correspondence.

From the start, Anne Scott-James drew a wide compass around so-called 'women's interests' – and she certainly never eschewed fashion, as her other self on *View* was obliged to. In the article introducing herself to the readers of *Picture Post* she explained:

I want to be useful. Women's lives today are peculiarly distracted. For our instincts and our circumstances pull in opposite ways. We want to spend: we're asked to save. We need more sleep: we've far less time for it. We want rather more food: there's less time to eat. We find that the war has created all sorts of new needs (from khaki socks for our husbands to thermos flasks for our shelters), just as most of our budgets are down and prices are up. How can we reconcile these needs? How can we be good citizens and still enjoy ourselves? How can we live attractively in these incredibly difficult days? The answer is by being practical. By learning how to do things well. By putting our brains into the

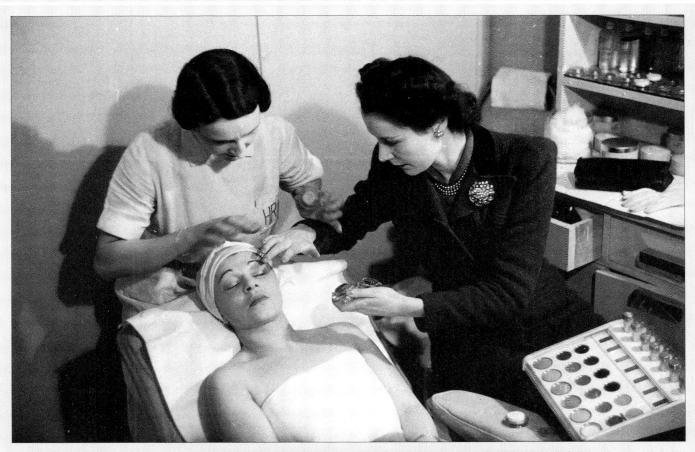

business of living. And this is where I want to help ... [The] problem will become more intense than it now is. You will have to be even more skilful with poor materials and I shall have to work even harder to round up practical ideas ... my job will be to help you to keep up with the times. Suppose, for the sake of argument, we are reduced to plain black woollen frocks for all. I shall show you how to twist a scarf round yours, how to clip a brooch on it, how to embroider a necklace on it, how to pin fresh flowers on it, so that you'll look fifty times smarter than your neighbour, who has taken no

trouble at all. Suppose there's a cold spell and no coal. I'll explore ways of keeping you warm without.

In the event, Anne Scott-James did even more for her readers than keeping up their morale and advising them on the nutritional value of nettles. She reported on the jobs women were taking in wartime – she tried being a conductor on a Midland Red bus herself – and recognized the battles and uncertainties they encountered in working and caring for a family during the days of war – and in facing a changed post-war world.

ABOVE LEFT: *Bessie Braddock visits Page Street, one of the inner-city areas due for clearance, where conditions are among the worst in the country.*
LEFT: *Mrs Braddock on the home front. At the house in Liverpool's Zig-Zag Road, where she lives with her husband and her sister – who is a professional bead-threader – and her family, Bessie Braddock shares the domestic chores.*

Battling Bessie Braddock

Bessie Braddock was elected Labour MP for the Exchange Division, Liverpool in 1945 – one of twenty-four women Members. Her majority was a narrow 551, but by 1951 the reputation of 'battling Bessie' for getting things done had pushed it up to nearly 7,000.

Mrs Braddock was born in a two-up, two-down terraced house in Kirkdale in 1899, into a fiercely political family. Indeed, her first outing at three weeks old was with her mother to a meeting of the ILP (Independent Labour Party). She was a founder-member of the Communist Party in Liverpool between 1919 and 1924, and before becoming an MP she was a City Councillor for twenty-four years.

The Member for Liverpool Exchange runs a surgery for her constituents every Saturday morning. 'Just tell me what you want,' she says, 'and I'll tell you what I can do.' And she battles on their behalf over everything – but particularly over housing. In her maiden speech she told the House of Commons, 'In industrial areas our people are living in flea-ridden, bug-ridden, rat-ridden, lousy hell-holes.'

ABOVE: *'Never show sympathy,' says Mrs Braddock as she takes note of a constituent's plight. Sympathy is fatal. Show just a little of it, and they keep you at it all day, when you ought to be doing something.'*

Photographed by Bert Hardy

A suitable job

'Wanted: Officer Material for peacetime work.' What happened to women who had been in the Forces, or had had other wartime jobs, when peace came? Some of them went back to the jobs they had had before the war, but some didn't want to do that, or had not had jobs pre-war. Selfridges, the London department store, decided that they could use in peacetime retailing some of the talents evident in wartime. So they set up a 'float' of women who were ex-officers, or NCOs, or who had shown 'marked ability' in other sorts of war work, and offered them a fast lane to the top. They were paid more than the regular staff – on potential rather than performance – received an hour and a half's training every morning and were moved around different departments to see where they were best suited. *Picture Post* followed a doctor's daughter from Kensington as she 'floated' round the store.

Photographed by Haywood Magee

LEFT: *Joan Quinn, demobilized, becomes part of the window display at Selfridges*

ABOVE: *'It suits you very well, madam.' A spell in millinery.*

ABOVE RIGHT: *And in hosiery.*

RIGHT: *And in perfumery, where Miss Quinn opts to settle. Some 'floats' have become under-buyers within a month of starting.*

Bluebell girls

'Tall dancers wanted: must be attractive – for long, interesting continental contract,' read the advertisement in *The Stage*. The audition was for Bluebell girls to dance at the Sistina Theatre in Rome, and the ten girls who fitted the bill would soon find themselves en route to Paris to meet the legendary 'Miss Bluebell', herself once a *Folies Bergère* dancer. They would then go on to Milan to rehearse, before making their débuts in Rome, high-stepping and swirling in the briefest of sequinned and plumed costumes, ogled by the audience, but always strictly chaperoned from the theatre to their modest *pension*.

Photographed by Grace Robertson

BELOW LEFT: *'It's abroad!' The wonders of Paris, glimpsed en route to Italy.*
BELOW RIGHT: *'So this is Italy.'*
BOTTOM: *Going through their paces at the Teatro Nuovo in Milan.*

RIGHT: *For Bluebell girls, good looks and deportment counted as much as dancing ability.*

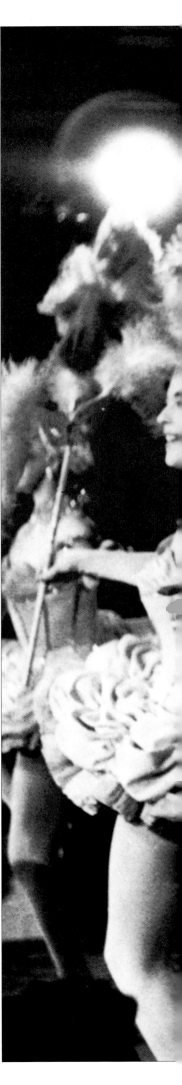

Anna Wickham: poet and landlady

In the living-room of the Hampstead house of the poet Anna Wickham hung a notice:

> Tour Bourgeoisie. Anna Wickham's Stabling for Poets, Artists and their Executives. Saddle your Pegasus here! Creative mood respected. Meals at all hours.

As a landlady, Anna Wickham may have respected the 'creative mood' in others; her own poems, however, record the continual frustration between women's endless domestic tasks and their need for expression.

> *If any ask why there's no great She-poet,*
> *Let him come and live with me, and he will know it;*
> *If I'd indite an ode or mend a sonnet,*
> *I must go and choose a dish or tie a bonnet...*

Picture Post paid a visit to Anna Wickham, who was 'celebrated in America, appreciated in France – mistress of words that sing and words that devastate, [yet] is still without full honour in her own country'. It followed her around the area of Hampstead, where she and her lodgers lived.

Photographed by Kurt Hutton

Too Much Washing
I plant my hope,
On my Irish view of water
And my Italian attitude to soap.
I am my father's daughter.

I bath by spells,
At holy wells;
I take my works
And wash them with the Turks;
Then without sin,
I disregard my skin...

Nervous Prostration

I married a man of the Croydon class
When I was twenty-two.
And I vex him, and he bores me
Till we don't know what to do!
And as I sit in his ordered house,
I feel I must sob or shriek,
To force a man of the Croydon class
To live, or to love, or to speak!

The Fresh Start

Two years now I have sat beneath a curse
And in a fury poured out frenzied verse, . . .
My dog is rabid, and my cat is lean,
And not a pot in this place is clean.
The locks have fallen from my hingeless
  doors,
And holes are in my credit and my floors . . .

TOP LEFT: *From the balcony of a department store restaurant Hilde Marchant and Lionel Birch 'make their preliminary recce', gazing down on the factories, shops, markets and dance halls.*

By way of evidence ... a student reading English at Leicester University (MIDDLE LEFT); *two workers at a Leicester clothing factory* (LEFT); *and a crooner with Percy Glover's Band* (ABOVE).

FAR RIGHT: *Leicester women work,* Picture Post *concludes – many of the 52,000 in the hosiery, clothing or footwear factories – and this is the secret of their 'prettiness'. Work gives them a 'pleasant independence ... a poise and a frank, natural air in their contact with young men.' This is why they have been able to perpetuate the legend that Leicester has the 'prettiest girls in England'.*

Is it true what they say about Leicester?

Following a series of nationwide beauty contests, the city of Leicester won the reputation of possessing the 'prettiest girls in England'. So in 1948 *Picture Post* writer Hilde Marchant went with fellow-journalist Lionel Birch and photographers Bert Hardy and Kurt Hutton, to find out: 'Is it true? And if so, what makes it so?'

January 15, 1941

PICTURE POST

NORWEGIAN GIRLS PLAY
MUD-FOOTBALL IN THE PARK

HULTON'S NATIONAL WEEKLY *In this issue:* **ON BOARD A WOOLWORTH AIRCRAFT CARRIER** 4D

JANUARY 15, 1941   Vol. 22. No. 3

TIME OFF

THE FIRST SEVEN YEARS OF *Picture Post*'s existence were years of crisis and war; the next five or six were a time of post-war austerity. It was important to remember that some things had been fun, and they would be fun again. The concept of time off became an important way of celebrating ordinary lives.

So *Picture Post* featured fairgrounds and circuses, seasides and holiday camps – or 'jolliday' camps as Butlins tried to christen its particular brand of non-stop regimented fun – flower shows and garden fêtes, dances and balls, pub outings and Sunday school treats. It played along with the necessary idea that wartime holidays at home were as much fun as a trip to the seaside:

> The war has brought the country to the town. The Cockney has
> found out that he can have as good a beano in London as in Brighton
> ... and that the same sun peels the skin off your nose at home as in
> Southend. For the first time Londoners have gone for their holiday –
> to London.

And when the war was over, and it was possible to admit that 'holidays-at-home were not one of wartime's most successful experiments', the magazine took up their legacy – street parties for children.

Women frequently played a dual role in the stories about leisure and holidays, and having fun. They were often the subject of the story – girls hitch-hiking to the south of France, taking a boat out on the Norfolk Broads, or going on cycling days out – but at the same time they were photographed in such a way as to provide some titillation for the readers. Every fairground story seemed to show girls coming down the helter-skelter, or on the big wheel, with their dresses blowing up in the wind; no seaside story seemed complete without a pretty girl artlessly posing in a swimsuit. And increasingly *Picture Post* seemed happy to collude with the star-making publicity machine by creating non-stories, when starlets went to Boulogne for the day, or 'welcomed the spring', or bought a hat.

But many time-off stories managed to catch precisely that feeling of snatched pleasure that constituted most women's 'free time', when they took a coach or a river bus and sang all the way to Southend, or Margate, or Clacton; or danced in the pub in the evening after a hard day's hop-picking.

Butlin's holiday camp

Butlin's first holiday camp opened at Skegness on the Lincolnshire coast in 1936. During the war Billy Butlin – dubbed 'the workers' Nash' – built three camps for the Admiralty to use, on the understanding that he could buy them back again at a fixed price when the war was over.

They formed the basis for Butlin's chain of seaside camps, which revolutionized post-war holidays for families – with so much laid on that mothers had a proper break, too. Grace Robertson took these photographs at Skegness in 1955.

ABOVE: *Music played through the camp's loudspeakers starts the day and swings it along.*

LEFT AND RIGHT: *'Is everyone happy?' Butlin's means Redcoats. Described as 'ice-breakers', they must have seemed like fun police to some campers, with their relentless determination that every holidaymaker must have fun, and be seen to be having fun, from dawn to dusk.*

BELOW LEFT: *The children are looked after and entertained.*
BELOW RIGHT: *And there is a free nappy service.*

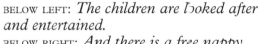

The bow women of England

July 1939 While the biggest peacetime army in British history was being trained, small bands of enthusiasts – many of them women – struggled to preserve the greatest weapon the British soldier had ever known. Archery had become a hobby.

August 1950 There were fifty archery clubs by the end of the war, but five years later there were 300 – with women shooting alongside men and frequently winning the world championship.

Photographed by Augustus Darwell and Slim Hewitt

An English garden, 1946

Mrs Nellie Neale would like to live in the country. But she doesn't. She lives in Hoxton, in London's East End. She stayed put, at the same address she has lived at since 1919, all through the Blitz – though her daughter was evacuated to the country. And during those war years she spent her time bringing the country to her small patch of the city. So now that peace has come, she can enjoy a veritable cottage garden of flowers, six ducks, eight chickens, a cockerel and a handful of rabbits, right here in her own back yard.

Photographed by Francis Reiss

Mothers' day off

The mothers of Bermondsey in London – the 'bearers, the raisers, the feeders, the washers-up, the packers-off-to-work, the tidiers-up-after' – had a day off. They went on a coach trip to Margate, and the photographer Grace Robertson – who had got to know them pretty well by then – went along too.

The pictures were published in *Picture Post* in September 1954, but forty years later nothing has diminished the exuberance of the women's day off.

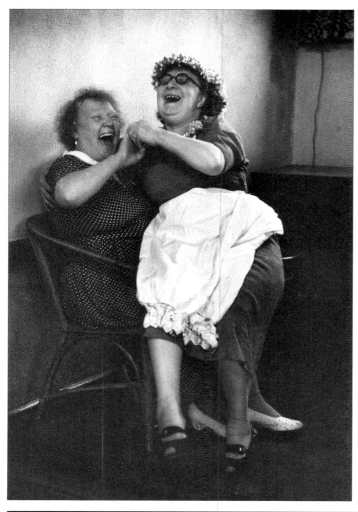

On the road

In the summer of 1953 two hard-up art students took to the road in a Romany cart and wandered around the Cotswolds, playing their guitar and singing on village greens and in pubs by way of a summer holiday.

TOP LEFT: *Travels with a cart-horse. The two London students set off for the lanes and farm tracks of rural England.*

TOP RIGHT: *Enduring the worst that the English weather can throw at them.*

ABOVE: *They sing blues and folk songs in village pubs. The villagers turn out to listen, some join in and some buy glasses of cider for the strolling minstrels.*

OPPOSITE TOP: *The girls bathe in the Windrush and sleep in barns.*

RIGHT: *Chicken in a pot and music round the camp fire on a warm summer's night.*

Photographed by Slim Hewitt

We go home with a Windmill girl

In 1950 *Picture Post* followed Pat Holden from her can-can life at London's non-stop revue theatre, the Windmill, to show that, however sexy and scantily dressed the dancers were on stage, at heart they were just nice, ordinary girls doing a job of work and hurrying home to see the family whenever they had a free moment. Pat Holden might be 'Margot' on stage and wear sequins and frou-frou frocks, but back home no one should 'take it for granted that private lives must necessarily reflect stage performances'.

Photographed by Haywood Magee

TOP LEFT: *'We Never Close.' Dancing a hula on stage at the Windmill Theatre.*
MIDDLE LEFT: *Back to Mum's cooking: Yorkshire pudding. Mrs Holden was once a dancer herself.*
BOTTOM LEFT: *Pontefract: home of liquorice cakes. Pat balances on the old city walls with a dancer's assurance.*
RIGHT: *Her brother Brian, who works at the local branch of Montagu Burton, the tailor, shows Pat his new bike.*
BELOW: *All the world's a stage: handstands in the back garden.*

Starlet to star

In 1950, when Audrey Hepburn was twenty, she was singing and dancing in a review called *Sauce Piquante* at the Cambridge Theatre. She 'caught the eye of the critics' – and of *Picture Post,* too. So in May that year they ran a 'pretty girl greets the spring' story, when they took Miss Hepburn to Kew Gardens, since, with all the rehearsing she had had to do for the revue, she had apparently missed out on the vernal equinox that year.

Five years later Audrey Hepburn was a star. *Picture Post* caught up with her again in Paris, where she was filming *Funny Face* with Fred Astaire.

Photographed by Bert Hardy

Ingrid Bergman in London

In 1949 the Swedish actress Ingrid Bergman was in London filming *Under Capricorn*, directed by Alfred Hitchcock. The scandal of her affair a year earlier with the director Roberto Rossellini meant that Hollywood was shunning Bergman. But *Picture Post* approved of her. It found her 'refreshing; she doesn't talk like a film star. She doesn't walk like a film star.' So they took her on a walkabout in London with Hitchcock, 'who was born within the sound of Bow Bells and married at Brompton Oratory'. They photographed the director and his leading lady sightseeing in the capital and, apparently, 'There was scarcely a passer-by who batted an eyelid.'

Photographed by Kurt Hutton

Wall-of-death rider

Sixteen-year-old Maureen Smith can't ride a bicycle – yet thirty times a day she dices with death on a 20-year-old Indian motorcycle at sixty miles an hour, clinging to the walls of the matchwood cylinder that is Southend's 'wall-of-death'. Previously Maureen helped her parents run their seaside boarding house. Then one lunchtime, when she was helping out in the ticket office, 'Tornado' Smith, who gave up taxi-driving to run the wall-of-death, suggested that she might like to try, and perched her on his handlebars while he lapped the 20-foot-high wall. Maureen's natural aptitude – and the fact that she had never learnt to ride the right way up – meant that within five weeks she was a solo star.

Photographed by Bert Hardy

The sculptor and the actress

Barbara Hepworth had an exhibition of her sculpture at London's Lefèvre Gallery in March 1950 prior to its despatch to Venice, where Hepworth was one of the two artists representing Britain at that year's *Biennale*. *Picture Post* took the 19-year-old actress, Claire Bloom, who was appearing in Anouilh's *Ring Round the Moon*, to the gallery, to give them an opportunity to pose the star against the sculpture – and talk about 'two talented women'.

Photographed by Haywood Magee

LEFT: *The actress as spectator: Claire Bloom studies Barbara Hepworth's sculpture, 'Biolith'.*

LEFT: *She contemplates 'Biocentric Form', on exhibition at a West End gallery.*

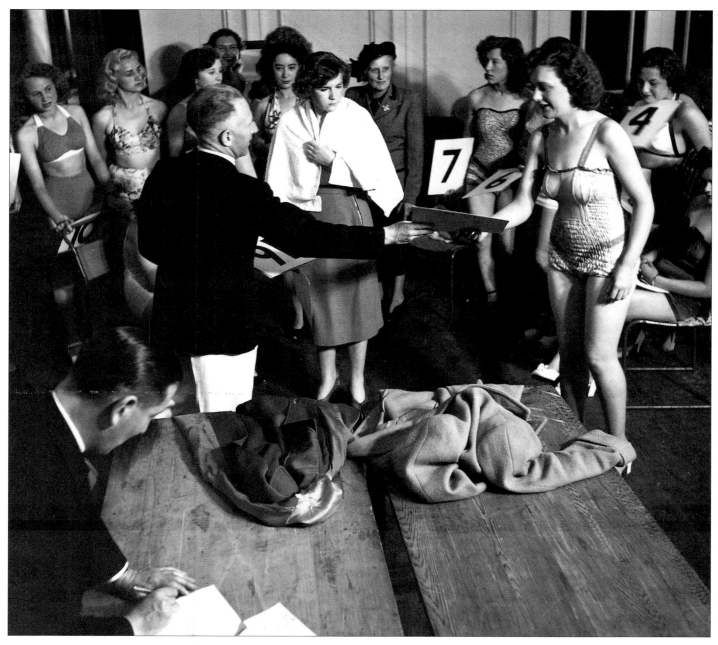

Beauty show

At 2.30 p.m. on an August Thursday in 1951, a Bolton shorthand typist who was on holiday on the Isle of Man arrived at the Villa Marina Gardens wearing her bathing costume under her frock. She had come to enter the Douglas Bathing Beauty Competition – strictly no padding allowed; judges' decision final.

FAR LEFT: *Numbers are handed out and final instructions given, and then it's on to the catwalk.*
LEFT: *The contestants parade and pivot under the appraising scrutiny of the official judges – and those who regard themselves as having an eye for this sort of thing.*

FAR LEFT: *Judgement time. The five women judges confer.*
MIDDLE LEFT: *Jean Stansfield of Bolton is Miss Greeba, 1951 (Greeba being a mountain on the Isle of Man). She gets a tumult of applause from all those in the audience of 6,000 who can see what's happening; a cheque for £5; a free tea; tickets for her and her boyfriend (who didn't come to the competition) for that night's Corporation Ball; a three-day holiday, all expenses paid, back on the Isle of Man in September; and the chance to enter the finals and maybe end up with a cheque for £100 and a sash bearing the legend 'Queen of Man'!*
LEFT: *Miss Greeba, 1951 poses for the local press, while the also-rans await their turn for the glare of local publicity.*

Photographed by George Douglas

***A visit to
the Tate***
Grace Robertson's
pictures of
women looking at
pictures, 1952.

We hitch-hiked to the sun on £5

Determined to get to the Riviera for a holiday, but short of money, two young English women decided to hitch-hike across France, reckoning on taking five days to get to St Tropez – and to do it on £5, all in (the year *was* 1954).

They managed – at a time when hitch-hiking was unusual for women and not apparently perceived as unwise – and offered some hints to *Picture Post* readers who might wish to follow in their footsteps.

Photographed by Maurice Ambler

● *Your rucksack is your badge of genuineness. Make sure drivers can see it . Wear it on your back.*

● *He didn't stop! But it's important to look hopeful until the car is out of sight. Some drivers have a change of heart down the road.*

● *Best to stand in the sun. And try to position yourself near a curve in the road, where cars have to slow down.*

● *Some lorry drivers like you up front in their cabs – they say the company helps keep them awake on long stretches. Others don't take passengers inside, but you're welcome to climb in the back.*

● *Always take advice when you can. A* gendarme *ponders the transport problem.*

● *The Object of the Whole Exercise – and money enough to stay for a week in the sun.*

PICTURE POST

GIRLS ARE TAKING OVER THE
BALLOON BARRAGE (see inside)

HULTON'S NATIONAL WEEKLY

In this issue:
SECOND FRONT: FOR and AGAINST
by TOM WINTRINGHAM and COMM. STEPHEN KING-HALL, M.P.

JUNE 13, 1942   Vol. 15.   No. 11

4D

WOMEN AT WAR

PICTURE POST was less than one year old when war broke out. The first issue after the declaration of hostilities on 3 September 1939 carried a double-page photograph of women standing, watching and seemingly listening, some of them crying. It was not possible to see what they were looking at. The poignancy lay in the row upon row of sombre, watchful faces. They were, in fact, watching their children being evacuated from London to avoid the bombs, which, it was believed, would soon threaten the capital. It was a potent image, as *Picture Post* made clear in its caption:

> The women of Britain. Thankfulness and sorrow struggle in their faces as they watch their children leave for the country. They bore the weight of the last Great War. They bear the weight of this war, too. And in France and in Poland, in Germany, there are thousands of other women on whom the burden of war lies just as heavily.

Throughout the war *Picture Post* did not forget this burden. It recognized that the Second World War was a people's war, and to a large extent that meant a women's war. The magazine chronicled the war effort of women in all its manifestations. It acted as a goad to the government on behalf of women. In March 1940, the MP Ellen Wilkinson was already charging:

> As Britain's war-machine gathers pace, the number of men available to keep it speeded up is falling. Millions of women will be needed to take the place of the men who are called up. What plans has the government got to fill them?

She went on to allege:

> We have a big labour reserve, $1\frac{1}{2}$ millions unemployed and an estimated 3 to 4 millions of women classed as 'unoccupied' – mainly married women. The question is, how can this huge labour force be organized to help in the national effort? . . .

It happened. By the end of the war seven and a half million women were mobilized, either in factories or in the auxiliary services.

But *Picture Post* looked ahead too. In 1942, Jennie Lee, MP, was unequivocal:

> The war creates a new life for women. What will be her life after the war? Equal pay for equal work, an equal chance in education. State help for the family. These are woman's minimum demands in a post-war world . . .

Wartime terminus

The mainline London stations in wartime – Paddington, Victoria and Waterloo – were a microcosm of the war itself. They were the places from which men and women in uniform left for war – and where they arrived for an all-too-short leave. The stations served as marshalling yards for children who were to be evacuated to the country, and for those whose schools had been moved out of London for the duration. And the war brought women to work in stations, doing jobs like ticket collecting, perching on ladders to carry out essential maintenance work, oiling and servicing the engines, and policing the station for 'incidents'.

Photographed by Bert Hardy

LEFT: *In charge – a small child guards his father's kit while his parents talk.*
BELOW: *A different war, a different uniform. Women take over the maintenance and cleaning of Paddington for the duration.*
RIGHT: *The troop train is now leaving . . .*

ABOVE: *Like the Portobello Road: a choice of pitchers and bowls – and devotional art.*

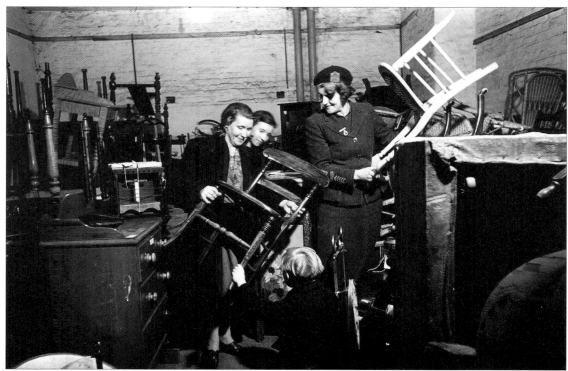

RIGHT: *A WVS member helps a 'customer' choose some furniture to rebuild her home.*

The store where everything is free

The Blitz turned whole areas of London – particularly East London – to rubble and debris. Those fortunate enough not to lose their lives often lost their homes and all their worldly goods. And then, in 1944, came the V1 and V2 bombs, which brought further devastation to the capital. Working among the victims of the raids, WVS workers thought up a national 'Good Neighbours' scheme, whereby people in the provinces, where for the most part they had escaped the V-bomb attacks, helped to provide furniture and household goods for the bombed-out Londoners. A provincial town or city would 'adopt' a London borough and fill a pantechnicon with donated goods to send to the capital. At the other end, the particular London borough's Rehousing Officer would draw up lists of people who had been re-housed – but who had lost everything. Families would then be invited to go 'shopping', without money, but with goods allocated on a points system, like rationing.

Shoreditch, where these pictures were taken, received seven pantechnicon loads from its 'adopter', Warwick, in early 1945 – and more were expected. There were 2,252 articles in the first load – it seemed like everything anyone could ever need, from mangles to ashtrays, babies' cradles to vegetable knives.

Photographed by Haywood Magee

ABOVE: *Mrs Hardy's haul. The Mayor of Shoreditch lends a hand to get it home.*

Singing for victory

We'll meet again, don't know where, don't know when,
But I know we'll meet again some sunny day,
Keep smiling through, just like you always do
Till the blue skies drive the dark clouds far away

sang Vera Lynn (RIGHT) week after week on the Forces' radio programme *Sincerely Yours*. Every week she received more than a thousand letters, and she sent off over eighty photographs of herself a day in answer to requests. Vera Lynn expressed the loneliness of millions – men and women away fighting – and of those who waited for them ... and worried. The War Office might have thought that this sentimentality was 'sapping the soldier's will to win and was a little dangerous', but to the men she was the 'Forces' sweetheart' – and she was often their sweetheart's sweetheart, too.

Anne Shelton (RIGHT) was the nearest Vera Lynn had to competition in the wartime singing stakes. She had a 'rich, boomy voice of the Sophie Tucker type. She will boop-a-doop as well as any if required, but seems to have more sense than to overdoop it,' *Picture Post* reported. Apart perhaps from 'We'll Meet Again' and 'The White Cliffs of Dover', the Second World War did not produce the memorable songs of the First. In fact, the most popular song of the war was the pre-war, German 'Lili Marlene', which was sung in the desert by both the Afrika Corps and the Eighth Army. Anne Shelton recorded an English version – and so, of course, did Marlene Dietrich.

Harvest festival

'There are few ceremonies more beautiful than that of the harvest,' wrote Vita Sackville-West in *Picture Post* in October 1941. 'It is beautiful to look at, and beautiful in its significance. It is simple and yet rich; modern and yet classic. It belongs to modern England as much as it does to ancient Greece and Rome. It means the same thing today as it always meant: it means that man has reaped the kindly fruits of the earth and is storing them against his need.'

To illustrate her words and to give a sense of praise offered for the 'earth's kindly fruits' in the midst of man's cruel war, *Picture Post* photographed the harvest festival – not in Sissinghurst in Kent, where Vita Sackville-West tended her own garden, but in the little village of Cassington in Oxfordshire.

Photographed by Kurt Hutton

Praise Him that He
gave the rain
To mature the
swelling grain . . .
And hath bid the
fruitful field
Crops of precious
increase yield
For His mercies still
endure
Ever faithful, ever
sure . . .

95

ABOVE: *Villagers young and old harvest their produce and bring it to the church.*
RIGHT: *'One of the things worth fighting for: the right to worship quietly in a village church.' The population of Cassington is fewer than 300. Twelve* men were killed in the 1914–18 war. In this war nearly seventy men and women are away fighting or on war work. The villagers gather to pray for them, as well as giving thanks for the harvest safely gathered in.

LEFT: *The defence of the suburbs. At the Women's Home Defence headquarters at Victory House, Leicester Square, Edith Summerskill (left) looks on as a Surbiton woman is signed up.*

LEFT AND BOTTOM LEFT: *The members meet once a week to learn how to fire rifles, revolvers and tommy guns, how to load and re-load as fast as possible, how to throw hand grenades, how to shoot from behind cover and how to take a pot-shot at a parachutist.*

Women sign on for Home Defence

After the fall of France in June 1940 the threat of invasion seemed very real. The role of the Home Guard as a back-up to the regular troops became vital. They would defend the home ground – and if necessary die on it. On 14 July 1940 Winston Churchill broadcast: 'Should the invader come, there will be no placid lying-down in submission before him, as we have seen, alas, in other countries.' For *Picture Post* the war would be lost if it wasn't a people's war – indeed, it was in the pages of the magazine that the term was coined – so it ran articles describing how civilians could resist invasion if they had the know-how to make Molotov cocktails, decapitate enemy motorcyclists with wire stretched across the road, and halt advancing

98

RIGHT: *If there was much sneering at the supposed broom-handle warfare of the male Home Guard, there was more than equal derision at that of the women – but male instructors were often prepared to give up time to teach the members, premises were frequently loaned without charge, and the Dorchester Hotel offered its ballroom at no cost for a fund-raising event.*

RIGHT: *In an effort to dispel probable reader disquiet at pictures of competently armed women,* Picture Post *stressed the defensive nature of the exercise – and evoked tragic pictures of France, where guns lay discarded at the roadside while women crouched unarmed in cellars.*

troops by scattering broken glass in their path. The owner of *Picture Post*, Sir Edward Hulton, financed a privately run Home Guard school at Osterley Park to turn the foot soldiers of 'Dad's Army' into guerrillas. So it was hardly surprising that the magazine took a particular interest in women's attempts to learn 'do-it-yourself war'. The Home Guard would not take women, so in December 1941 Dr Edith Summerskill, a Labour MP, founded the Women's Home Defence. Anyone could join – and by the beginning of 1942 there were well over fifty units in different parts of the country. The women reporters of Fleet Street had their own unit, as did the women workers at the Gillette razor-blade factory.

Photographed by Kurt Hutton

BELOW: *Mrs Griggs gets up at 6.30 a.m. to start the milking. 'In peacetime, she ran the dairy, but the cowman did the milking. In wartime, she has to be prepared to turn her hand to everything' – and she can.*

BELOW: *'She's as good a judge of a bird as the poulterer.' Tending the poultry (White Leghorns and Rhode Island Reds) is one of Mrs Griggs's main jobs on the farm. She sells eggs – and sometimes fowl, too.*

RIGHT: *Far from the coal and coke rations, Mrs Griggs and her daughters collect driftwood on the Cornish seashore. 'Breeding is a natural function on a farm ... a farmer's wife is not ... shy of having plenty of children ... Economically speaking, a farm baby is not another body to house and another mouth to feed, but a future "hand". Country children make themselves useful at a very young age ... Little girls are often good cooks at twelve or fourteen.'*

The farmer's wife

A countrywoman's life in wartime might seem an enviable one. Far from night-time raids and 'making do' in devastated towns and cities, less constrained by ration books and points systems, the rhythms of her life might seem less violated than those of her urban sisters.

As part of the war effort, *Picture Post* had been eager to remind its readers what they were fighting the war to preserve: the heritage of the British way of life embedded in the gentle beauties of the British – and particularly the English – countryside and its

ways. Yet clearly, in the eyes of *Picture Post*, rural values were in some way under attack towards the end of the war. Afraid, perhaps, of a post-war generation of modernized, urbanized women – whose lives were dedicated to consumerism, whose horizons were bounded by the 'all-electric kitchenette and the cinema', and who would inhabit a plasticized world of convenience-living and 2.4 children, with the illusory benefits of 'independence' on others' terms – its woman's editor, Anne Scott-James, went to the north coast of Cornwall to visit a farmer's wife and remind its readers of a world they could lose.

Mrs Griggs of Tremedda Farm near St Ives worked very hard, but she was the key figure in the life of the farm. She had not succumbed to the lure of the easy life of the 'townee' and become 'an unskilled worker, easily replaced'. Rather, she had made the traditional tasks of a wife and mother her power base. 'Her farmhouse is the hub round which the whole business of the farm revolves. The men of the business are largely dependent on her department and respect her efficiency ... Her social duties are considerable. She is an important person in the village.'

ABOVE: *'The farmer's wife still takes pleasure in cooking on a lavish Victorian scale, and at her table the grand tradition of English cookery still survives. The war has curtailed her menus, but she still expects to cook dinner for a dozen hungry people a day.'*

LEFT: *Farm work is very hard on clothes and there's always mending to do. At the end of a 15-hour-day's work around the farm, Mrs Griggs and her mother, Mrs Dow, catch up with the patching and darning.*

'In every part of the country, the farmer's wife works in this gruelling way. She has little leisure at any time of her life, and when still young, care and hard work imprint character lines on her face. But she has the supreme compensation of working at her own family business, with all the stimulus that independence gives. She makes her own plans. She reaps her own results. The townswoman need not pity her too much . . .'

Photographed by Leonard McCombe

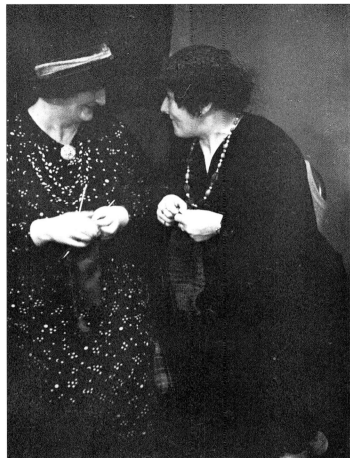

Socks for soldiers

Nearly everyone was knitting – or so it seemed – in 1940 ... socks for soldiers, scarves for sailors, comforters, gloves, woolly hats for servicemen and -women. Women's political clubs were transformed into knitting circles, churches organized knitting parties and women knitted wherever they were – at home, in friends' houses, in cinemas and shelters, on buses and trams. But no one was doing the job more thoroughly than the 400 members of the Women's Work Guild of Keswick in Cumberland.

Photographed by Gerti Deutsch

Wartime dance hall

Young lady dancing with a soldier
Feeling stern peaty cloth with your slight hand ...
So very happy to be dancing with the patriotic male ...
You have forgotten
Deliberately ...
Last month your partner was a shipping clerk ...

PHYLLIS SHAND ALLFREY

In a world at war, dancing became a craze, a relaxation and a respite, a chance for romance, friendship – and for forgetting. Every city in Britain seemed to boast at least one dance hall. At the Royal Opera House, Covent Garden, a band played on a revolving stage where the world's greatest opera singers had performed, and twice a day the house was packed with couples quickstepping, waltzing and foxtrotting to the music of bands such as Henry Hall, Victor Sylvester's Ballroom Orchestra or Ivy Benson. It was the same at the Astoria in Charing Cross Road, at the Hammersmith Palais, Green's Playhouse Ballroom in Glasgow, Sherry's in Brighton, the Tower Ballroom, Blackpool and many more, where servicemen and -women on leave – many far from home, families and friends – could meet each other and civilians, too, to talk, dance and drink – lemonade, since most dance halls were not licensed.

Photographed by Leonard McCombe

ATS gives soldiers a lesson

In the Second World War every soldier was issued with a *hussif*. It contained buttons, six, brass; thread, khaki, fifty yards – and a thimble. It had to be present and correct at every kit inspection. Then Eastern Command came up with a revolutionary idea. They would teach the men how to *use* this object. So each week during their initial training, the men were marched off to a hut where forty of them sat in semi-circles while half-a-dozen ATS women taught them that torn and worn uniform could, and should, be mended. And taught the soldiers how to do it. Themselves.

Photographed by Haywood Magee

RIGHT: *Through the eye of a needle …*
BELOW: *'I can't reach back there, and I can't take them off here.' Running repairs that defeat the object of the exercise.*

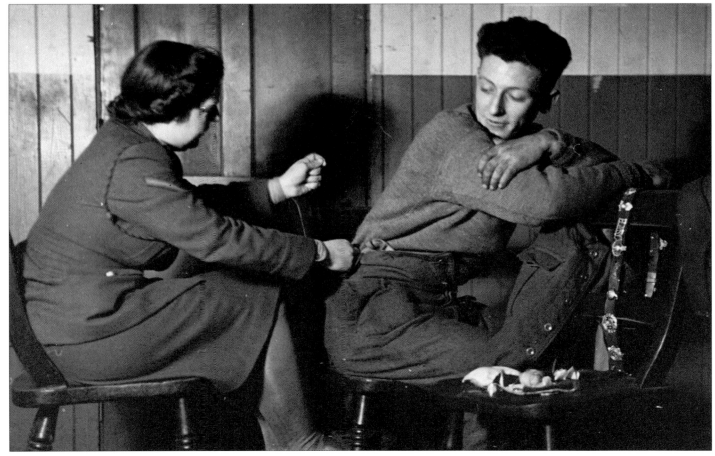

Ellen in office

The only woman Socialist in the wartime government, Ellen Wilkinson had been an organizer for women's suffrage in Manchester and a trade union organizer. She entered parliament in 1924, and was Member for Jarrow from 1935. After taking part in the Jarrow march against unemployment with 200 constituents in 1936, she wrote a book about it – *The Town That Was Murdered.*

In June 1940 Winston Churchill brought 'red Ellen' into the National Government as Parliamentary Secretary to the Ministry of Pensions, with special responsibility for war-service grants to fighting men. She was also in charge of the provision of air-raid shelters, and after the war was appointed Minister of Education in Attlee's Labour government.

Photographed by Kurt Hutton

ABOVE: *The new members of the ATS take a country walk near their training camp at Reading.*
LEFT: *Odessa Gittens, a 32-year-old school teacher from Barbados, is enthusiastic about London. 'The big city is stealing into my heart,' she is reported as saying.*
RIGHT: *Georgy Masson, who was born in Oxford, left Britain in 1930 and worked as a stenographer at the Ford motor depot in Trinidad. Now she's back in Britain and being measured for her military uniform.*

West Indian girls join the ATS

Thirty women from the Caribbean volunteered to come to Britain to join the Auxiliary Training Service. They arrived in late October 1943 to a cold and war-torn Britain. The War Office had long resisted the acceptance of women of colour into the British Forces and the group that arrived was racially mixed. Anxious to forestall any possible prejudice, *Picture Post* pointed out what an asset the women would be and the sacrifice they were making – 'They haven't come because they need a job; in fact, most of them had excellent jobs over there. They're all educated beyond School Certificate Standard and some of them were school mistresses before they joined up; one was a dressmaker, one was a dental assistant, another a radio operator; most of the others were stenographers in lawyers' offices and department stores.'

Photographed by Leonard McCombe

The seaside takes off its war-paint

By the summer of 1944 the war in Europe had begun to move over the horizon. The Normandy landings in June that year were pushing the German forces back across the Continent to the point from which the Panzers had started to roll five long years before. The threat of invasion was deemed to be over. The defences were breached, the barbed wire rolled back, and that summer the British reclaimed their beaches. Summer holidays start here.

Photographed by Leonard McCombe

111

Never tell the men, they will only
laugh and say
What use would a woman be!
But I read the war news through,
every day;
It means my honour to me,
Making the crops to grow,
And so, and so,
Said the farm woman:
But I bruise easy.

'The Farm Woman, 1942',
NAOMI MITCHISON

Photographed by Bert Hardy and Haywood Magee

The Women's Land Army

The Women's Land Army was hard work. The lure of the land attracted many who fancied fresh air and an outdoor life, but the reality was a 48-hour week, back-breaking physical labour in all weathers for low pay, with often unwelcoming farmers – and their wives – who were disgruntled at losing their regular labourers to the military and did not reckon that some slip of a town girl would be much in the way of compensation. But that didn't seem to stop women from applying – the Land Army expanded from 20,000 in 1941 to 80,000 in 1944.

Art school in Lakeland

During the Second World War, the Royal College of Art was evacuated to the Lake District. The new generation of artists – on the whole they were younger than pre-war students, and there were more women – lived and worked in a close community. Like those other creative artists before them, the Lakeland poets, they drew inspiration from the beautiful landscape, fashioned what they needed from what they could find – but missed the stimulus of museums, libraries, galleries and the wider artistic community that the metropolis offered, even in wartime.

ABOVE RIGHT: *A study in concentration.*

RIGHT: *A portrait class. A few models make the trek from London, but mostly the students paint local characters in stoical pose.*

RIGHT: *Landscape with figures.*

FAR RIGHT: *'Just a little more shadow here.' A masterclass.*

Photographed by Kurt Hutton

How to welcome a soldier home

A few weeks before the end of the Second World War, Sergeant Jim Ford of the Rifles Brigade came home from fighting in the Middle East to Druid Street, Bermondsey, in London's East End. He had been away at war for four years and nine months – and he didn't know quite what to expect when he came back. Since Sgt Ford had been away, his wife Betty had worked in a factory, joined the WAAF and now had a clerical job with the Ministry of Work – and she had established quite a life for herself. So she too wondered how it would be, now that her husband was home again after nearly five years away.

ABOVE: *Off to the station to meet the troop train – and anxiously scan the advancing greatcoats.*

TOP RIGHT: *A soldier's welcome. The Fords had been married for only eighteen months when Jim was posted overseas in 1940.*

MIDDLE RIGHT: *Bunting in Bermondsey for a hero of El Alamein.*

RIGHT: *Everyone gathers round the piano in the front room to celebrate – and leave it until tomorrow to see how the Fords will be able to pick up the threads of their lives together, in a world that is nearly at peace.*

RIGHT: *After the Warsaw rising of 1944, the Germans moved out the population and blew up the city, block by block. The Russians drove them out before Warsaw was completely razed – but nevertheless nearly nine-tenths of the city was left a wasteland. The housing shortage continues to be acute, even though a massive rebuilding programme was initiated. Ella and Jurek Kopek and their two small children live in a rebuilt block in the Mokotow district of the city.*

RIGHT: *Ella cooks Polish food, supervised by her husband's aunt.*

RIGHT: *Nowyswiat, once a street of grand hotels and expensive shops. Now shopkeepers trade in spaces carved out of the rubble – and there is little to sell.*

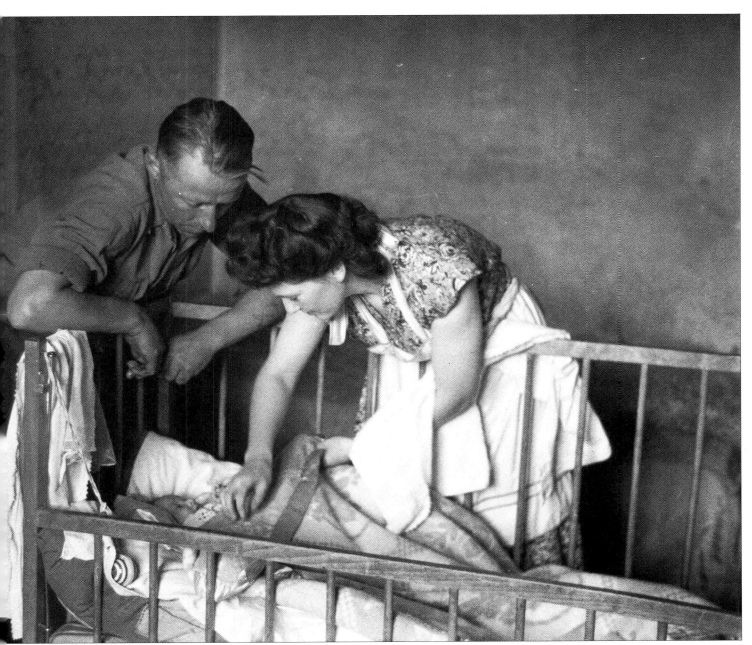

Country of hard work

Ella Kopka was born Ella Mulligan of Glasgow. During the war she married a Polish soldier, Jurek, and in 1946 they returned to Poland to live in Warsaw. The story of Ella's daily life in war-ravaged Poland was the focus of the first article in *Picture Post*'s exploration of life behind the 'Iron Curtain'.

Photographed by Bert Hardy

ABOVE: *Jurek works as a lorry driver for a newspaper company. The four Kopeks share their two-roomed flat with Jurek's aunt and a cousin.*
LEFT: *The church where Chopin's heart was buried. Ella shows her 4-year-old son, Eddie, the statue of Christ carrying His cross to Calvary bearing the sins of the world, in the city that lies at the heart of Europe's reconstruction.*

PICTURE POST

GRACIE FIELDS, HER NEPHEW, AND A TORTOISE

HULTON'S NATIONAL WEEKLY

In this Issue:
THE BIRTH OF A MAN

OCTOBER 29, 1938   Vol. 1. No. 5

3D

MOTHERS AND CHILDREN

PICTURE POST was in favour of babies. Children represented the future, and in wartime they became of particular concern, their safety paramount. The government's edicts on mass evacuation from the cities on the outbreak of war were strongly supported by the magazine, which pronounced that 'the best thing that's come out of the war' was the fact that city children, who 'until now had seen nothing but towns, houses, pavements, buses ... never knew grass grew like this'.

In the post-war world, as far as *Picture Post* was concerned, children were the litmus test of the government's promise of a better Britain. The magazine ran campaigns for the provision of more nursery schools, visited establishments of progressive education – picturing Zoë, the determined and self-regulating small daughter of A.S. Neil of Summerhill – and schools for children with special needs, often featuring photographs taken by women photographers – Gerti Deutsch, Edith Tudor Craig or Merlyn Severn.

Being somewhat ambivalent in its attitude towards women, *Picture Post* was particularly so when it came to mothers. On the one hand, photo-stories welcomed the return to peace as a golden opportunity for women to return to the home and train their daughters in the intuitive womanly arts; on the other, it welcomed the age of the expert with scientific theories of child-rearing, and recommended clinics and classes in babycare and child management, both to present mothers and to those who would one day set out on that path.

Picture Post was a magazine that wanted to appeal to both men and women readers. Features about mothers and children, either offering advice ('I am in touch with experts of every kind of infant welfare, and would be pleased to consult them on your behalf,' wrote Anne Scott-James in 1941) or a glimpse of how it was for others ('The Good Quads are Growing Up', 'Family of Twenty', 'I Am an Unmarried Mother', 'How to be a Father'), counted strongly in the 'women's interest' camp. But such stories were part of a broader perspective – *Picture Post* families might be concerned about the rising cost of children's clothes, but they were also presumed to be interested in experiments in communal living; in babysitting schemes being run by the community; and in how children would adjust to returning to the cities after their enforced wartime rural sojourn.

Are baby shows necessary?

August was the month for baby shows. They were held at seaside resorts, holiday camps, agricultural shows, village fêtes, and billed as a 'special attraction', with silver cups and trophies awarded for the 'best baby'. The shows drew proud mothers – and a big crowd – and they swelled the coffers of whatever organization was putting them on.

But the babies didn't like them. They hated being prodded and pushed and weighed. The mothers didn't like them if their baby wasn't judged the winner – it could sour relations between friends and neighbours for years. And increasingly the experts didn't like them, either. They thought that the 'best' baby was an odd concept. It showed little about mothercraft and treated children like prize cattle to be fattened up. So *Picture Post* went along to photograph a dying custom – and to fuel the argument that that's precisely what it should be.

Photographed by Haywood Magee and Thurston Hopkins

122

Growing up

It was feared that during the Second World War domestic arts were being lost. The handing-down of female wisdom from mother to daughter had not been possible when homes were being evacuated or mothers out working in war industries. *Picture Post* reported on two different training schemes with but a single aim – to re-domesticate women and professionalize their home-making skills.

At Kensington High School in London it was questioned how much school time should be given to 'Latin and Algebra and Greek mythology; how much to household and technical subjects the children are likely to need in later life?' In the term after they had taken their School Certificate at sixteen, the girls embarked on a course in child welfare. Some of the girls intended to work as nurses or nursery teachers, but in most cases it was 'training them for the real job in life many of them hope to undertake – marriage and motherhood ... It has been proved over and over again that these are the subjects in which most girls are naturally interested, [though] obviously a few will turn towards more academic pursuits, [and] a few will devote their lives to business or professional work.'

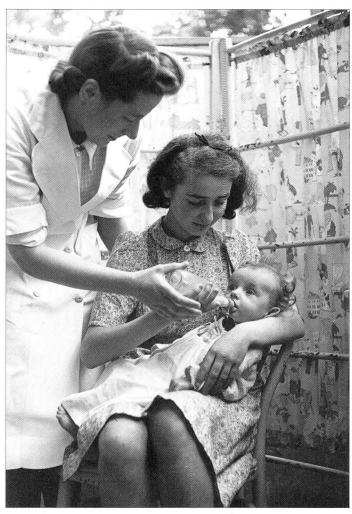

TOP: *They start with a rubber doll ...*
ABOVE: *And progress to a real baby.*

Photographed by Kurt Hutton

123

RIGHT: *How can I run a home on my husband's £5 wage? Starting to find the answer. The girls come from factory, shop and office. 'Even putting on a pinny is an unusual experience for some of them.'*
ABOVE: *Miss Sansom has been running the village store for forty years, so she can give the novice housekeepers some advice about provisions.*
LEFT: *The cottage has been deliberately chosen because of its inconvenience. The girls learn that 'domestic comfort isn't just laid on but needs creating'. There is a shortfall of cooking equipment, and meals have to be very ingeniously planned.*

At the end of the war, several home-making courses were tried out. The ATS ran a practical course for girls 'who have been cut off from home life for six years. Arranging flowers, making cushions and curtains, and cooking for four instead of four hundred, will turn their barrack-trained minds to a softer domestic scene.' Several local county council schools had fully-equipped flats attached to their cookery departments, and youth organizations were turning their pre-service instruction into courses for brides and future mothers. One of the most ambitious of these was run by the Girls' Training Corps, which took over a cottage in Dorset and, with a grant from the Ministry of Education, ran fortnightly courses enabling girls to learn how to 'turn dead rooms, still cookers and a barren pantry into a living home'. Perhaps it was hardly surprising that at the end of the week, struggling over how to feed a family of four on washing day, one of the girls asked, 'Is there a course on how to get a rich man who can afford a laundry and a couple of servants?'

Photographed by Merlyn Severn

The sixth form visits Paris

The sixth form of Great Malvern Girls' school was taken on an educational trip to Paris in the autumn of 1946. Since this was the first time that most of them had been out of England, the girls walked around the capital in their school uniform revelling in the 'foreignness' of France.

Photographed by S. Kleboe

TOP LEFT: *'Attention, Garçon!' The school sixth arrives in Paris.*

TOP RIGHT: *A schoolgirl sends a postcard home.*

RIGHT: *Art in the galleries. A visit to the Louvre: the Malvern school sixth clusters round the statue of the Venus de Milo.*

ABOVE: *Art in the streets. The perpetual tourist attraction of the place du Tertre, Montmartre.*

ABOVE LEFT: *This is going to be an entirely new experience, too.*

Grace Robertson

Grace Robertson became a photographer for *Picture Post* through perseverance. During the post-war years of food shortages she was queuing outside a butcher's shop in 1948 – she was seventeen at the time – when:

> [my] attention was caught by two women in the doorway engaged in intimate conversation. When one of them whispered a confidence in the other's ear, this brought on an explosion of laughter so intense that they had to clutch each other for support. One girl was blonde, with a Veronica Lake hairstyle that kept falling over her eyes; the other had come shopping in curlers .. I watched, fascinated, without immediately understanding why. Then out of the blue I realized that they would have made a marvellous photograph, *if I had had a camera in my hand!*

Grace Robertson knew from that moment not only that she was going to be a photographer, but that she wanted to be a *Picture Post* photographer.

I hurried home and dragged copies of *Picture Post* from a cupboard. I spread them over the floor. Everywhere faces stared back at me: war criminals, statesmen, tribal chiefs, evangelists, and again and again, the faces of ordinary men and women ... I said to myself, this is what I want to do. I want to take pictures like these.

She acquired a Leica camera, borrowed books on photography, taught herself how to develop films – and submitted some of her work to *Picture Post*, using the name 'Dick Muir'. Her father, the journalist Fyfe Robertson, was working for the magazine

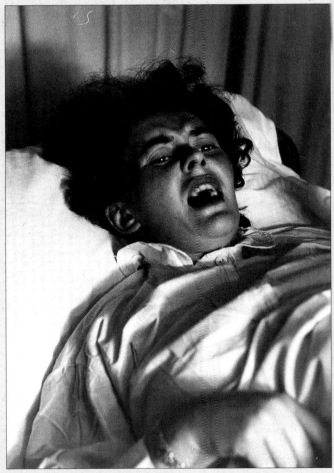

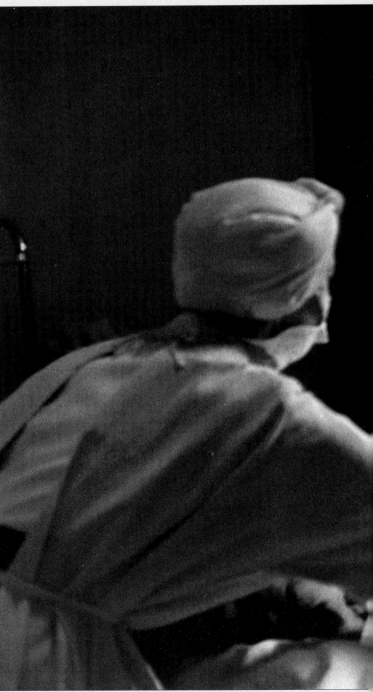

and Grace wanted no favours, and was anxious that a young woman might not seem to have the worldly experience that she felt informed the magazine's pictures. Her first attempts were rejected – but with the advice, 'These show promise. Persevere, young man.' She did, and her first photo-spread, showing her sister, Elizabeth, doing her homework, was published in *Picture Post* in 1951 – under her own name.

'It has often been said that there is no story in happiness' is an adage that Grace Robertson's work disproves. Her special gift is for the 'quiet stories', those photo-essays that take patience and powers of subtle observation. And she was always drawn to photographing women, and particularly 'stroppy women', survivors of two world wars and the Depression. Her most famous story for *Picture Post*, 'Mothers' day off' (see pp. 70–3), was one the magazine could see no point in when she proposed the idea: but her photographs convinced the editor that he had been wrong; there *is* a story in happiness – in the right hands.

But there was one moment of woman's most intense feelings that *Picture Post* thought its readers might not wish to share: childbirth. Grace Robertson's 1955 photo-story was killed at the last moment.

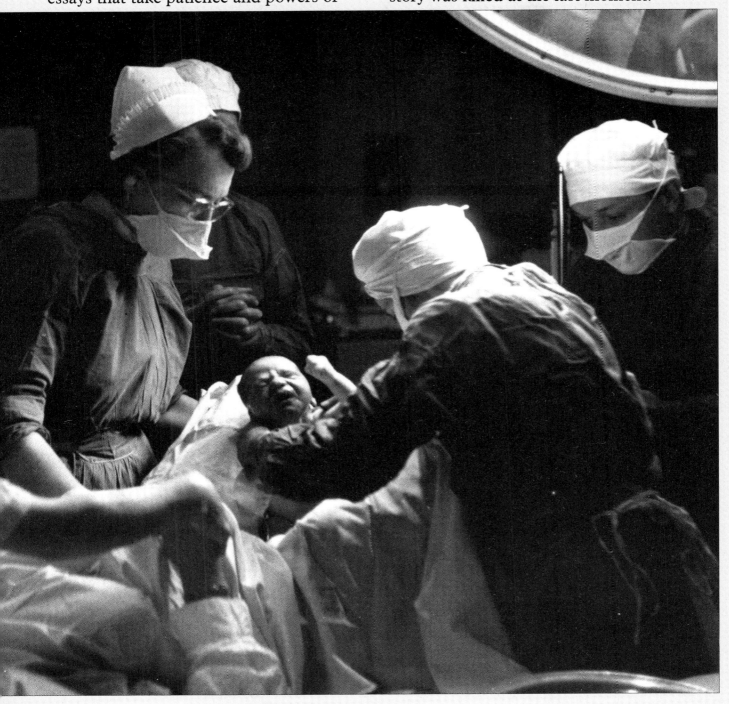

A family of twenty

Mrs Hudson has just had her twentieth baby. He is already an uncle to her older daughters' children, and the entire family – fifteen surviving Hudsons and six grandchildren – lives together in a terraced house in Holloway, north London. The Hudsons always wanted a large family – even though Mr Hudson was earning only ten shillings a week when they married in 1927. Now he earns £9, plus a little overtime, as a kitchen cabinet sprayer, and they receive £2 16s family allowance. But with the family devouring fifty-two pounds of potatoes a week, fourteen loaves of bread, and each of the younger children getting pocket money every Saturday, that doesn't stretch very far.

Photographed by Kurt Hutton

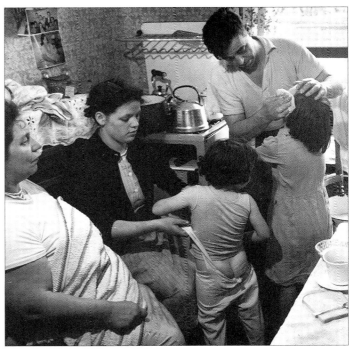

ABOVE: *A seat in the stalls.*
TOP RIGHT: *Ready for school, hair brushed and faces scrubbed.*
MIDDLE RIGHT: *The Hudsons on parade.*
RIGHT: *Three in a bed and no room to roll over.*

ABOVE: *Pay day, and a caution from their father not to blow all their pocket money at once.*

RIGHT: *Saturday night is treat-time, with ice lollies for all.*

133

Motherhood

An 'average' British housewife with two children was estimated to work at least a 12-hour day in 1956. As *Picture Post* pointed out, 'Few men work as long and many can barely visualize what that ambiguous term "housewives' duties" really involves. They include cooking, cleaning, scrubbing, window-cleaning, house decorating, washing, ironing, first-aid, nursing, carrying coal, humping laundry, sewing, mending, patching, darning, cleaning sinks and drains, helping neighbours, caring for pets and polishing.' And mothers caring for young children hardly get tea breaks or sick leave – and there's no overtime pay.

To make the point, *Picture Post* followed an 'average' British housewife and mother with three small children and a baby on an 'average day' at her Norfolk home – and not surprisingly subtitled the story 'The Job with the Hundred-Hour Week'.

Motherhood – a new model

It was the age of the expert; child mortality and malnutrition were believed to be the product not only of poor housing and inadequate diet, but also of lack of knowledge about 'mothercraft'. So training classes were started in the pre-war years, to which mothers could bring their babies and learn the best way to care for them. And for years, it seems, it was mothers only who took on the job of early parenting. But at Kingston-upon-Thames in 1939 the photographer Gerti Deutsch found that fathers were encouraged, too. In fact, sometimes at the Saturday afternoon classes the fathers outnumbered the mothers.

LEFT: *Mr Hann gets to grips with his daughter, Wendy.*
BELOW: *'Motherhood classes' announces the blackboard – and fathers assemble.*

136

University women

When, in 1849, Elizabeth Jessie Reid founded the 'Ladies' College of Bedford Square' she intended that its higher education would encourage the 'moral and intellectual character of women'. It was the oldest university college for women. A hundred years later *Picture Post* spent a day there, and concluded that the college 'more than fulfils its founder's wildest dreams'.

BELOW LEFT: *In 1949 the all-woman college has 830 students. It is housed in Regent's Park – though it was evacuated to Cambridge during the war, when the BBC took over its quarters.*
BOTTOM: *The library: Bedford College has a strong tradition of education in the social sciences and training in social work.*
BELOW: *Zoology students specialize in freshwater studies on the Regent's Park lake.*

Photographed by Kurt Hutton

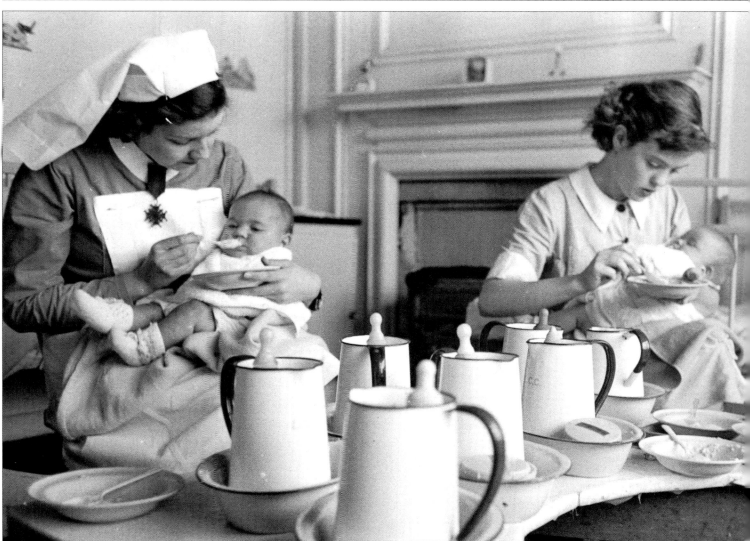

ABOVE: *The London Diocesan Council for Moral Welfare runs several mother-and-baby homes. At some, the girl arrives some six weeks before her baby is due and stays for six weeks after, while she makes up her mind if her baby should be adopted, or if she wants to try to keep it. 'She is not persuaded in any way ... but it is quite a decision' – and often one she has to make entirely on her own. At the home that* Picture Post *visited, thirteen out of the thirty-one mothers had decided on adoption – the rest 'were prepared to face the struggle'. At other homes, mothers who have decided to keep their babies, but who have no accommodation, live for a year while they try to find work and somewhere to live with a baby. No woman is 'turned out unless she has a reasonable chance of success with her child ... but there are time limits.'*

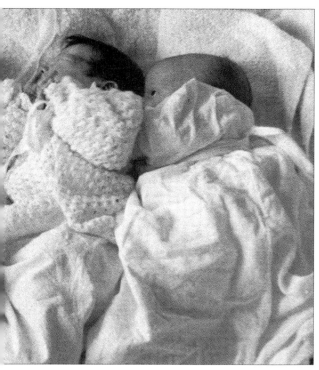

LEFT: 'Mary' was a working-class girl of eighteen when she became pregnant. Her father (her mother had died when she was a baby) stood by her after he had got over 'the great shock'. 'Mary' wanted to keep her baby – whose own father had 'long ago ceased to call'.

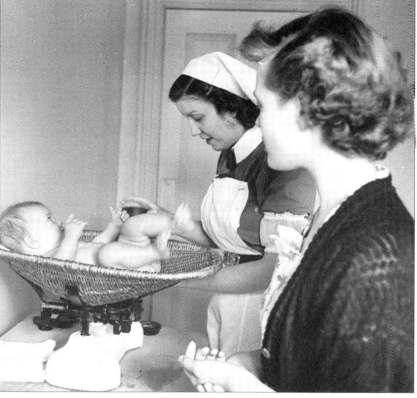

LEFT: 'Mary' took a job as a day nurse at the home where she had her baby, looking after the babies of other unmarried mothers. But, Picture Post assured its readers, 'Mary' has a 'sense of wrong ... the way she will repay the understanding [of her family] is by bringing up her baby, and by working her way back into society'.

Photographed by
Joseph McKeown

I fight to keep my baby

There were 33,000 babies born out of wedlock in 1954. Society was still very hard on the mothers of illegitimate babies – if not on the fathers. Words like 'shame' and 'disgrace' were commonplace, and the National Council for the Unmarried Mother and Her Child, founded in 1918, was often castigated for 'encouraging immorality and wickedness'.

Hilde Marchant wrote the story of 'Mary' and her baby 'Ann' (not their real names, but they were identified in photographs) for *Picture Post*, both to 'throw light on a subject that is not always discussed as fully or openly as it deserves' and to encourage girls who were facing abandonment by the fathers of their babies and hostility from their own parents, that there *was* an alternative to the dangerous, illegal back-street abortion – help was available.

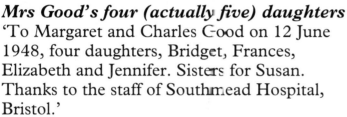

Mrs Good's four (actually five) daughters

'To Margaret and Charles Good on 12 June 1948, four daughters, Bridget, Frances, Elizabeth and Jennifer. Sisters for Susan. Thanks to the staff of Southmead Hospital, Bristol.'

The Good girls were Britain's first surviving quads. *Picture Post* took an interest in them from the start. It photographed the proud parents taking the babies home to the adjoining houses that Sodbury District Council had allotted to the Goods, when it was obvious that Margaret and her £5-a-week farm-labourer husband were not just increasing their family with twins, as they had been led to expect. And the magazine took a rain-check when the quads were sixteen months old, and called again to record their first day at school.

Photographed by Kurt Hutton

TOP LEFT: *No hand-me-downs for the Goods quads. Four of everything at the same time is what they have hanging in the wardrobe.*
TOP RIGHT: *Elizabeth, Jennifer, Frances and Bridget pose for a staircase photo-call – at least three of them do. Elizabeth decides to scale the heights.*
RIGHT: *The quads perambulate while big sister Susan rides postilion on her tricycle.*
FAR RIGHT: *Mass consumption. It's a two-person job to keep the quads fed and watered. Mrs Good and the children's nurse administer lunch.*

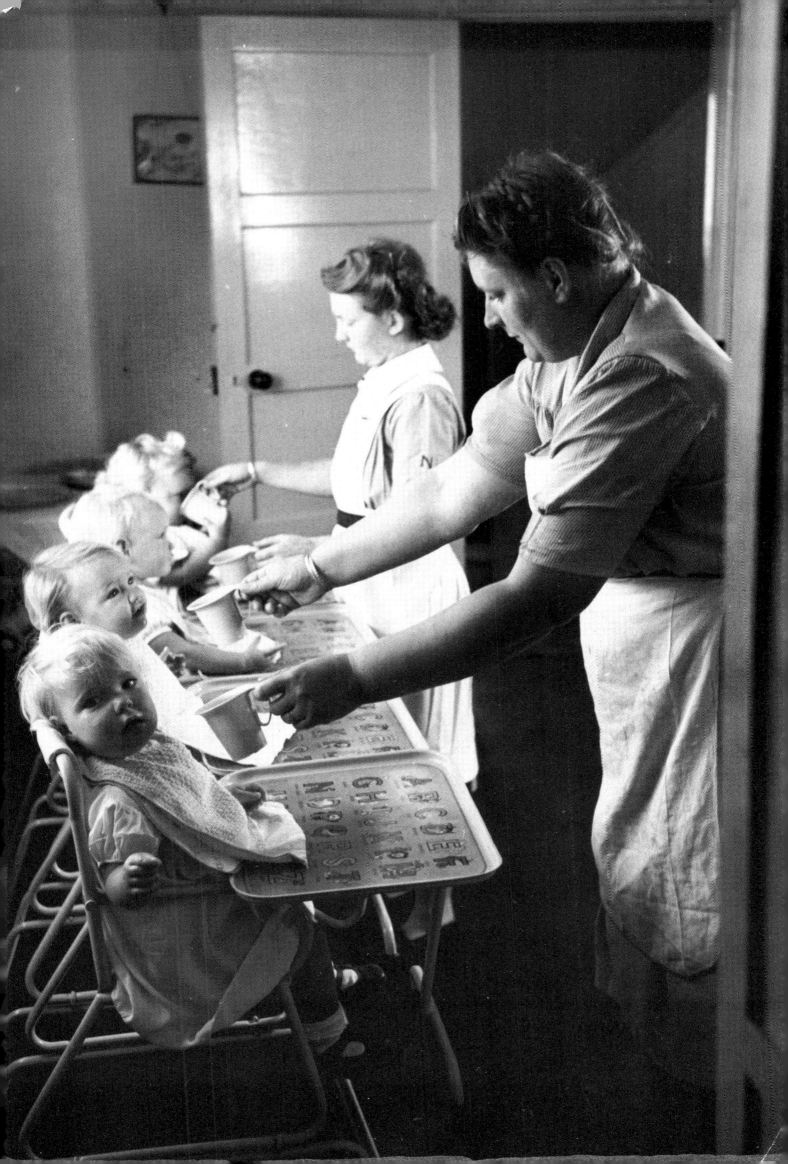

LEFT: *Uniform dressing. But the system breaks down for the quad on the end.*

ABOVE: *First steps in education. Susan Good, aged seven, takes her four little sisters to join her at Westerleigh village school, near Bristol, in June 1953.*

WITHDRAWN

Advertisements that appeared in the wartime pages of Picture Post, *reflecting and encouraging women in their wartime roles.*